JOKES

WARNING! ADULT CONTENT INSIDE

for grown-ups!

Aura

How do you keep a blonde amused?

Give her a piece of paper with PTO written on both sides

What is a man's idea of safe sex?

A padded headboard

Darth Vader and Luke Skywalker were sitting under the family Christmas tree on Christmas Eve when Darth turned to Luke and said, "I know what you're getting for Christmas tomorrow."
"How do you know that?" asked Luke.
Vader replied, "Because I felt your presents."

ॐ ॐ ॐ ॐ

Our local football team has announced that their new sponsors are to be Tampax tampons. The chairman believes this is a sensible move as the club are going through a very bad period.

What's the definition of mixed feelings?

A lawyer driving over a cliff in your new car

ॐ ॐ ॐ ॐ

Frog in a pub: A pint of beer please.
Barman: That will be £100 and I must say we don't get many frogs in here.
Frog: At those prices I'm not surprised!

A man and a woman in bed were just about to engage in the dirty deed when the man said, "Could we try something different tonight?"

"Ok, what do you want me to do?" asked his lover.

The man replied, "Take this glass of water, sit on top of the wardrobe and flick the water on the bed. That's the rain. Bang your left foot on the wardrobe door. That's the thunder. Flick the bedroom light on and off. That's the lightning."

His lover duly obliged but after ten minutes she was getting more than a little bored.

"Aren't you going to make love to me?" she asked.

"What, in this bloody weather?" replied the man.

A man was sitting by his wife, who lay in a hospital bed in a coma. As he adjusted her nightdress, he accidentally brushed her right nipple. He gasped as his wife let out a sigh. He quickly informed the doctor of the breakthrough and the doctor said, "Perhaps other forms of sexual stimulation would bring her out of her coma. I suggest you pull this blind around the bed and try oral sex."

"I'm willing to give it a try," said the husband.

The doctor left the pair to preserve the woman's dignity when five minutes later an alarm rang from behind the screen and the heart monitor ceased to bleep. The husband called the doctor who immediately attempted to resuscitate his wife. The doctor returned from behind the screen and said, "I'm sorry sir, I'm afraid your wife is dead. Have you any idea what happened?"

"I'm not sure," said the husband. "I think she must have choked."

A man walked into a bar with his arm in a sling, two black eyes and a split lip.
"What happened to you?" asked the barman
"The next-door neighbour caught me in bed with his wife and beat me senseless," said the man.
"Didn't you fight back?" asked the barman.
"No," replied the battered man, "he had a baseball bat in his hand."
"Didn't you have anything in your hand?" asked the barman.
"Yes," replied the man, "his wife's breast, but it wasn't much use in a fight."

———————

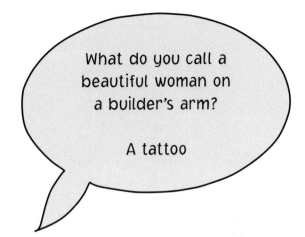

What do you call a beautiful woman on a builder's arm?

A tattoo

A man was driving along a country lane when he collided with a skunk. He got out of his car and carried the shivering, injured animal back inside. "It's cold," said the man to his wife, "put it between your legs to warm it up."
"What about the smell?" she asked.
"Just stick a match up each of its nostrils and it'll be fine."

ॐ ॐ ॐ ॐ

What's six inches long,
three inches wide and drives
women crazy?

A £50 note

ॐ ॐ ॐ ॐ

**Why don't elephants eat
penguins?**

**Because they can't get the
wrappers off**

**A nurse appeared from behind
a screen carrying a pan of
boiling water, swiftly followed
by a man clutching his
reddened manhood, screaming
in agony. A doctor witnessing
the scene shook his head
ruefully and said to the nurse,
"No nurse, you misunderstood.
I told you to prick his boil."**

———————

A woman was trying hard to get
the ketchup to come out of the
bottle. During her struggle the
phone rang so she asked her
four-year-old daughter to answer it.
"It's the vicar, Mummy," the
child said. Then she added,
"Mummy can't come to the phone
right now. She's hitting the bottle."

What's pink, wrinkly and hangs out your boxer shorts?

Your grandmother

ॐ ॐ ॐ ॐ

What's the difference between roast beef and pea soup?

Any idiot can roast beef

_____

Bob, Frank and Eddy went everywhere together and particularly enjoyed their regular pub-crawls. One night they arranged to meet in the Dog and Duck, and Bob arrived early.

On his arrival he paid a visit to the pub's toilet when tragedy struck, as he spontaneously combusted.

A customer found his body, charred beyond recognition. When Frank and Eddy walked into the pub, the pair were asked to identify the body. Frank proceeded to remove Bob's trousers and turned him over onto his stomach.

"That's not Bob," said Frank. "How do you know that?" a voice piped up. "I can answer that," said Eddy. "Whenever we are out drinking everybody always says, here comes Bob with the two arseholes."

Why did the ref call a penalty in the leper ice hockey game?

Because there was a face off in the corner

ॐ ॐ ॐ ॐ

How do you save a taxman from drowning?

Take your foot off his head

A survey has showed that when builders go for a drink after work they talk about football. When supervisors go for a drink they talk about tennis and when company executives go for a drink after work they talk about golf. The survey concluded that the higher up you are in the management chain the smaller your balls get.

———————

A girl is walking down a woodland path when she notices a little green man sitting on a toadstool with his head between his knees.
"Are you a goblin?" asks the little girl.
"No, I've just got a headache."

Why did God create Adam before Eve?

Because he didn't want Eve telling him how to make Adam

Patient: Doctor, doctor I've got a bowl of strawberries stuck up my bum.

Doctor: I've got some cream for that.

A husband and wife were sunbathing on a nudist beach when a wasp swooped down and disappeared into the woman's nether regions. Unable to get the wasp out, they dressed, jumped into their car and drove to the nearest surgery. The doctor examined the woman and said, "It looks like the wasp has gone up a long way but I have a suggestion. Take this honey and smear some on the end of your penis, then insert your member in your wife to try to entice the wasp out."

The husband followed the instructions and mounted his wife with his honey-smeared willy. After a couple of minutes the husband began to thrust violently and his wife screamed, "Stop, stop you're going too fast!"

"Change of plan," replied the husband, " I'm going to drown the little bugger."

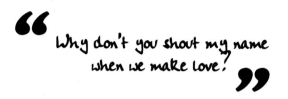

"Why don't you shout my name when we make love?"

"I don't want to wake you up."

A man returned from the chemist's with a new brand of Olympic condoms that came in three colours – gold, silver and bronze.

"I'm going to wear the gold condom tonight," announced the man.

"Can't you wear the silver one?" his partner asked, "and come second for a change?"

———

Two parrots are sitting on a perch. One says to the other, "Do you smell fish?"

ॐ ॐ ॐ ॐ

"A toothbrush and a roll of toilet paper were chatting in the bathroom.

The toothbrush said to the toilet paper, "I must have the worst job in the world. Every night and morning I get covered with a gungy foam and stuck under the hot water tap. I get thrust inside smelly mouths and rubbed against half-eaten food and furry teeth.

My head is covered in saliva then I am thrown in a glass where I have to sit around all day waiting for the next time I'm used."

The toilet paper looked at the toothbrush and said, "Yeah, right, whatever."

Three ducks were swimming on a pond when a policeman arrested them and took them in front of the judge.

The first duck walked up. Judge: "What's your name?"

First duck: "My name is Duck."

Judge: "What did you do?"

Duck: "I didn't do anything. I was just swimming around blowing bubbles."

Judge: "There's nothing wrong with that. You can go."

The second duck walked up. Judge: "What's your name?"

Second duck: "My name is Duck-Duck."

Judge: "What did you do?"

Duck-Duck: "I didn't do anything. I was just swimming around blowing bubbles."

The judge with puzzled look on his face: "There's nothing wrong with that. You can go."

The third duck walked up.

Judge: "I bet your name is Duck-Duck-Duck."

Third duck: "Nope. My name is Bubbles."

John called round to see his friend Tom. "Hi John, how are you?"
"Just fine," said John, "how's the wife?"
"Oh, she's dead," replied Tom.
"I don't believe it," said John. "When did that happen?"
"Last week. I buried her in the back garden," said Tom. "Come on, I'll show you." They walked through to the back garden, where Tom showed his friend his wife's grave. A freshly dug patch of ground stood in the middle of the garden and sticking out of the ground was the backside of his dead wife. John looked down and said, "I hope you don't mind me asking, but why have you left her backside sticking out of the ground?" Tom replied, "Because I needed somewhere to park my bike."

What do you call a deer with no eyes?

No-Eye Deer

What do you call a deer with no eyes and no legs?

Still No-Eye Deer

_____

What do you call a man with no arms or legs that can swim the English Channel?

Clever Dick

ॐॐॐॐ

Wife: Darling, we have a problem with the car.
Husband: What's the problem?
Wife: The carburettor is flooded.
Husband: How do you know?
Wife: The car's in the river.

Why don't women blink during foreplay?

Because they don't have the time

ॐ ॐ ॐ ॐ

What is the difference between a hedgehog and a Porsche?

Hedgehogs have the pricks on the outside

What is a zebra?

Twenty-five sizes larger than an A bra!

ॐ ॐ ॐ ॐ

**Patient: Doctor, doctor I have a serious problem.
Doctor: Tell me all about it.
Patient: My bowels open at 7 o'clock on the dot every single morning.
Doctor: That sounds regular. I don't see what your problem is.
Patient: I don't get up until 9 o'clock!**

———————

Why did the blonde fail her driving test?

Every time the car stopped she jumped into the back seat

ॐ ॐ ॐ ॐ

What is the definition of a tree?

Something that stands still for years and then leaps out on unsuspecting women drivers

Doctor, I think I'm a dog.
How long have you felt
this way?
Ever since I was a puppy!

Client: How much do you charge?
Lawyer: £100 a question.
Client: Can I ask you three questions?
Lawyer: Certainly, now what's your third question?

66 A man walks into a pub with a slab of tarmac on his head and says, "Two beers please, one for me and one for the road." 99

> **What's the difference between a woman and a battery?**

> **A battery has a positive side.**

A skeleton walks into a bar and orders a pint of lager and a mop

ॐ ॐ ॐ ॐ

Patient: Doctor, doctor, I think my wife is dead.
Doctor: What makes you think that?
Patient: The sex is still the same but the ironing is piling up.

———————

What do you get if you cross a rooster with an owl?

A cock that stays up all night

"

Ted and Tom were the two sole survivors of a shipwreck and were floating in a lifeboat somewhere in the Pacific Ocean. They noticed a lamp bobbing towards them. Ted picked up the lamp, gave it a polish and out popped a genie.

"You may have one wish," said the genie.
Without thinking Ted blurted out, "I wish all the water in the ocean could turn to beer."

The genie clapped his hands and immediately the surrounding water was turned into beer. Tom looked at Ted and said, "You do realize, this means we'll have to piss in the boat!"

"

19

A teacher walked into the class and said, "Today, children, we are going to do some maths problems. Tell me, Billy, if three birds are on a fence and you shoot one of them how many would be left?"

Billy replied, "None, the shot bird would fall to the ground and the other two birds would be frightened away by the noise."

The teacher said, "The actual answer is two, but I like the way you're thinking."

"Let me ask you a question," said Billy. "Three women are eating a lollipop, one is licking it, one is crunching it and one is sucking it. Which of the three women is married?"

"I'm not sure Billy, I'll say the one who is sucking it," said the teacher.

"No," said Billy, "the correct answer is the one wearing the wedding ring, but I like the way you're thinking!"

On her first day in the jungle, Jane sees the muscular Tarzan striding purposefully towards a tree. He removes his loincloth, grabs the tree by the trunk, inserts his manhood into a hole in the tree and begins pumping away furiously. Jane is quite taken aback but at the same time curiously aroused. She quickly removes her clothes, runs naked up to Tarzan, taps him on the shoulder and lays on the floor with her legs asunder. Tarzan approaches her and gives her a forceful kick between her legs, "What the hell did you do that for?" screams Jane.
Tarzan replies, "Checking for wasps."

What's a Hindu?

Lays eggs

ॐ ॐ ॐ ॐ

A couple are dining at a fish restaurant when the woman begins to choke on a trout bone. The waiter rushes over, bends her over the table, pulls down her knickers and then licks the woman's backside. Immediately the stricken woman coughs out the fish bone and collapses into her chair. The waiter returns to the kitchen and the chef says to him, "That was amazing you saved that woman's life."
"Yes," said the waiter, "the hind lick manoeuvre works every time!"

The local sheriff was looking for a deputy, so Gomer, who was not exactly the sharpest nail in the bucket, applied for the job.

"Okay," the sheriff drawled, "Gomer, what is 1 and 1?" "Eleven," he replied. The sheriff thought to himself, "That's not what I meant, but he's right."

"Which two days of the week start with the letter 'T'?" "Today and tomorrow." The sheriff was again surprised that Gomer supplied a correct answer that he had never thought of himself.

"Now Gomer, listen carefully: Who killed Abraham Lincoln?" Gomer looked a little surprised himself, then thought really hard for a minute and finally admitted, "I don't know."

"Well, why don't you go home and work on that one for a while?" So, Gomer wandered over to the barbershop where his pals were waiting to hear the results of the interview. Gomer was exultant.

"It went great! First day on the job and I'm already working on a murder case!"

**What's the difference
between an oral and
a rectal thermometer?**

The taste

ও৽ও৽ও৽ও৽

What's the difference between
a pizza and a drummer?

A pizza can feed a family of four

_____

**What's white and slides
across the disco floor?**

Come dancing

A man moves from Ireland to
New York City, leaving two of
his best friends behind. To keep
their tradition of nightly drinks
alive, each evening he goes into
an Irish-style pub and orders
three pints. After a month of this,
the bartender becomes curious,
and asks the man what he's
doing. Touched by the story, the
bartender has the three pints
ready for the man every time he
comes in. One day, the man tells
the bartender to only give him
two pints. "My condolences,"
says the bartender, thinking
that one of the man's friends
has died. "No, no," says
the man, "they're both still
alive. I've just quit drinking."

ও৽ও৽ও৽ও৽

When I'm gone you'll never find another man like me.

What makes you think I'd want another man like you!

What do you call a Skoda with no wheels?

A skip

৯৯৯৯

A blonde walks into a chemist's and says to the assistant, "Could you help me please? My boyfriend suffers from the most terrible dandruff." "I suggest you try giving him Head and Shoulders," said the assistant. "OK," said the blonde with a puzzled frown, "but how do you give shoulders?"

_____

"Two pieces of string were standing outside a pub. The first piece walked into the pub and ordered a pint of lager.

The landlord looked at him and bawled, "Out you go, we don't serve pieces of string in here." The string trooped out of the pub, dejected.

The second piece of string said, "Let me have a go," and proceeded to ruffle up the top of his head into a tangled mess. He strode purposefully into the pub and ordered a pint of lager. The landlord eyed him suspiciously and said, "Are you a piece of string?"

To which he replied, "No, I'm a frayed knot."

What have you got if you have one large green ball in one hand and another large green ball in the other hand?

The undivided attention of the Jolly Green Giant

What do you get if you cross a fart with a boomerang?

A smell that keeps coming back

ॐॐॐॐ

What's the difference between a woman suffering from PMT and a Rottweiler?

Lipstick

What's the difference between a G spot and a golf ball?

A man will spend hours searching for a golf ball

———————

ॐॐॐॐ

Did you hear about the vegetarian cannibal who only ate Swedes?

What's the difference between a girlfriend and a wife?

About 60 lbs

ॐॐॐॐ

Why don't sharks attack lawyers?

Professional courtesy

_____

Where would you find an upside down tortoise?

Wherever you left it

ॐ ॐ ॐ ॐ

Teacher: Timmy can you spell bowling?

Timmy: B-O-E-L-L-I-N-G

Teacher: That's the worst spell of bowling I have ever seen

How can you tell if a politician is lying?

Their lips move

_____

66 Patient: Doctor, doctor, I've broken my leg in three places.
Doctor: Make sure you don't go back to any of them. 99

An Englishman, an Irishman and a Mormon were in a pub chatting about their families.

The Englishman said, "I've fathered 11 children and it's like having my own football team."

The Irishman said, "I've fathered 15 children and it's like having my own rugby union team."

The Mormon said, "I've got 18 wives and it's like having my own golf course!"

࿐ ࿐ ࿐ ࿐

What's the difference between a broken clock and a football referee?

The clock is right at least twice a day

The latest Barbie doll, Divorced Barbie, has hit the shops. It comes with all the usual accessories plus half of everything that Ken owns.

———————

What goes boing, boing, bang?

A kangaroo in a minefield

What has three balls and comes from outer space?

E.T. the extra testicle

Did you hear about the Wild West outlaw known as The Brown Paper Kid? He was wanted dead or alive for rustling

An old man went to the doctor complaining of impotency. The doctor examined him before saying, "Take this bottle of pills, take three daily and come back next week to see if they're working."

The following week the old man returned to the doctor who asked, "Any improvement?"

The man shook his head and said, "I tried with my right hand, then with my left hand and then my wife tried with her right hand and then with her left hand. The milkman arrived and he tried with his left hand and then his right hand."

"You mean you let the milkman have a go?" asked the doctor incredulously.

"Yes," replied the old man "but we still couldn't get the bloody top off the bottle."

A carpet layer had just finished fitting carpet for a lady. He stepped out for a smoke, only to realize he'd lost his cigarettes. In the middle of the room he saw a bump. "No sense pulling up the entire floor for one pack of smokes," he said to himself. He proceeded to get out his hammer and flatten the lump. As he was cleaning up, the lady came in. "Here," she said, handing him his pack of cigarettes. "I found these in the hallway. Now," she said, "if only I could find my parakeet."

ॐॐॐॐ

A hamburger walks into a bar, and the bartender says, "We don't serve food here."

Two hydrogen atoms walk into a bar. One says, "I think I've lost an electron." The other says, "Are you sure?" The first says, "Yes, I'm positive."

_____

A drunk is standing on a street corner, when a policeman passes by, and says, "What do you think you're doing?" The drunk says, "I heard the world goes around every 24 hours, and I'm waiting for my house. Won't be long now, there goes my neighbour."

ॐॐॐॐ

A man hasn't been feeling well, so he goes to his doctor for a check-up. Afterwards, the doctor gives him the results. "I'm afraid I have some very bad news," he says. "You're dying, and you don't have much time left."
"Oh, that's terrible!" says the man. "How long have I got?"
"Ten," the doctor says sadly.
"Ten?" the man asks. "Ten what? Months? Weeks? What?"
The doctor interrupts, "Nine..."

What's the difference between an oooh and an aaah?

About four inches

Tom had a problem getting up in the morning and was always late for work. His boss had threatened to fire him if he didn't do something about it. So Tom went to his doctor who gave him a pill and told him to take it before he went to bed. Tom slept well, and in fact, beat the alarm in the morning. He had his breakfast and drove to work. "Boss," he said, "the pill worked!" "That's great," said the boss, "but where were you yesterday?"

"

A man walked into a pub with an ostrich and a cat. He walked up to the bar and said, "Three pints of beer please." The landlord started to pour the beers when the cat piped up, "Don't think I'm paying for these!" The man shook his head and said, "No, I'll get them." The trio sat drinking their beer and 20 minutes later were faced with three empty glasses. "Three more pints please," the man said and again the cat wailed, "Don't look in my direction for any money." The ostrich looked at the cat and said, "It's OK, I'll get this round." The landlord was amused by these exchanges and said to the man, "I hope you don't mind me asking, but why are you out drinking with an ostrich and a cat which if you don't mind me saying, is a bit of a skinflint?"

"It's a long story," said the man. "I bought a lamp at an auction and when I took it home and cleaned it a genie appeared before me and told me he would grant me one wish."

"What did you wish for?"

The man replied, "I wished for a bird with long legs and a tight pussy."

"

Two men were talking in a pub when one said to the other, "My wife's off to the Caribbean next week." "Jamaica?" asked his friend "No, she chose it herself," he replied.

ঙ্কঙ্কঙ্কঙ্ক

Patient: Doctor, doctor, I've just returned from holiday and I've got the most terrible sunburn on my legs. I can't sleep at night because the duvet is irritating the burns.
Doctor: Take this cream for the sunburn, a sleeping tablet to help you sleep and a Viagra tablet.
Patient: What's the Viagra tablet for?
Doctor: That will help keep the duvet off your legs.

Little Billy was late for school one day and eventually arrived halfway through Mrs Robinson's history lesson. The teacher fixed him with a cold glare and asked, "Where have you been until this time, Billy?"
"I'm sorry I'm late Miss but my father got burnt," replied Billy.
"I'm sorry to hear that, is it serious?" said Mrs Robinson.
"Yes," said Billy, "they don't piss about at the crematorium!"

———————

Did you hear that Count Dracula was dismissed from his post at the Transylvanian blood bank for drinking on the job?

What do you get if you cross Lassie with a Doberman?

A dog that rips you to bits and then goes for help

ॐॐॐॐ

What is the insensitive part at the base of the penis called?

The man

**Two men were getting dressed after a game of squash when one of the men noticed his opponent stepping into a pair of French knickers.
"Forgive me for asking," he said, "how long have you been wearing French knickers?"
His opponent replied, "Ever since my wife found a pair on the backseat of the car."**

ॐॐॐॐ

Two blondes are playing with a torch. One of them switches the torch on and shines it up to the ceiling and says to the other, "I bet you can't climb to the top of that."
"You must think I'm stupid," her friend replies, "As soon as I get to the top you'll turn it off."

Two missionaries were captured by a tribe of cannibals in deepest Africa. The leader of the tribe approached them licking his lips and said, "It is our custom to spare our captives if they're able to perform two tasks. Your first task is to go into the jungle and return with ten items of the same fruit."

The missionaries sped off into the jungle and ten minutes later one of them returned holding ten grapes in his hand. The cannibal leader said to him, "Your second task is to insert each of the grapes up your backside without making a single noise. But should you fail then we will eat you."

The missionary began inserting the grapes up his backside and was just about to insert the tenth when he burst out laughing. The cannibal smiled and said, "Sorry but you have failed the test and now we are going to eat you. But before we eat you could you tell me why you started laughing on the tenth grape?"

The missionary replied, "I've just seen my friend coming, and he's carrying melons!"

A guy can't get an erection. He goes to the doctor who tells him the muscles at the base of his penis are broken and there's nothing he can do unless he's willing to try experimental surgery. The doctor tells him they take the muscles from the base of am elephant's trunk, insert them in the base of his penis, and hope for the best. The guy says that sounds pretty scary but the thought of never having sex again is even scarier, so go ahead.

The doctor performs the surgery and about six weeks later gives the man the go ahead to "try out his new equipment". The guy takes his girlfriend out to dinner. While at dinner he starts feeling an incredible pressure in his pants. It gets unbearable and he figures no one can see him so he undoes his pants. No sooner does he do this than his penis pops out, rolls across the table, grabs a dinner roll and disappears back into his pants. His girlfriend sits in shock for a few moments and then gets a sly look on her face.

She says, "That was pretty cool! Can you do it again?" With his eyes watering and a painful expression on his face, he says, "Probably, but I don't know if I can fit another roll up my ass."

What's the connection between Viagra and Disneyland?

Both make you wait two hours for a one-minute ride

ॐ ॐ ॐ ॐ

What do air and sex have in common?

They're no big deal unless you're not getting any

A nun, a priest, an Irishman, a Jew, a Scotsman, a rabbi and a blonde walk into a bar. The bartender looks at them and asks, "Is this some kind of joke?"

_____

If your father isn't rich, you're unlucky. If your father-in-law isn't rich, you're stupid.

One summer evening during a violent thunderstorm, a mother was tucking her son into bed. She was about to turn off the light when he asked with a tremor in his voice, "Mummy, will you sleep with me tonight?" The mother smiled and gave him a reassuring hug. "I can't dear," she said. "I have to sleep in daddy's room." A long silence was broken at last by his shaky little voice: "The big sissy."

How do you make a hormone?

Refuse to pay her

**What does PMS really
stand for?**

Permissible Man Slaughter

_____

What's the difference between a
bull and an orchestra?

The bull has the horns in the
front and the asshole in the back

Two kangaroos live in a zoo
pen surrounded by a 20-foot-
high wall. One morning both
kangaroos are seen wandering
around the zoo and are quickly
captured and put back into
their pen. As a result the wall is
raised to 40 feet. However, the
following morning both
kangaroos are found outside
their pen enjoying a stroll. As
a result the wall is raised to
60 feet. One kangaroo turns to
the other and says, "How high
do you think they will keep
building this wall to?"
"I don't know," says the second
kangaroo, "it depends how long
it is before they figure out
they're not locking the gate."

_____

ॐॐॐॐ

Charles Dickens walks into a bar and orders a martini. The bartender asks, "Olive or twist?"

How many men does it take to open a can of beer?

None, it should be open by the time she brings it to the sofa

ॐॐॐॐ

_____

Paul was strolling down the street when he noticed an approaching funeral procession. He became puzzled when he saw two hearses followed by a man with a Dalmatian dog, who in turn was being followed by hundreds of men walking in single file. Feeling curious he walked up to the man with the dog and asked, "Whose funeral is this?" The man replied, "It's for my wife and my mother-in-law."
"How did they die?" asked Paul.

"The dog bit them and they developed rabies. They died within days of each other," the man told him.

"Do you think I could borrow that dog?" asked Paul.
"Join the queue!" said the man.

A taxi driver was coming to the end of his shift when he was flagged down by a nun. She climbed into his cab and sat on the back seat and he observed her intently through his rear view mirror. The nun noticed the driver's attentions and asked him, "Is there anything you want to ask me, my son?" The taxi driver gulped before replying, "This is going to sound dreadful, but I have always had a fantasy of receiving oral sex from a nun."

The nun didn't appear to be at all shocked and said, "I will make your fantasy come true if you can meet two conditions. The first is that you are Catholic and the second is that you are a bachelor." The taxi driver nodded his head vigorously and said, "I am Catholic and I am a bachelor."

The nun smiled and climbed into the front seat before fulfilling the taxi driver's fantasy. Ten minutes later the taxi driver had a huge smile on his face but was racked with guilt and said to the nun, "Sister, I have a confession to make. I lied to you. I am actually a married Protestant with six children."

"That's alright," said the nun, "I have a confession too. My name is Fred and I'm on my way to a fancy dress party."

What's the difference between pink and purple?

The grip

৵৵৵৵

Two men sat at a restaurant table reading the menu when the waitress approached them. "Can I take your orders now gentlemen?" she said in a cheery voice.
"Yes Miss, I would like a quickie," said the first man. The waitress slapped him round the face and stormed off, furious.
The man's dining companion looked at him disapprovingly and said, "What kind of idiot are you, it's pronounced quiche!"

Two convicts were sentenced to be executed on the same day. The prison warden walked into their cell and said to the first convict, "After the Last Rites have been administered do you have any final requests?"
"Yes, I am great lover of party music and the last song I would like to hear before my death is Agadoo," he replied.
The warden approached the second convict and said, "Do you have any final requests after the Last Rites have been administered?"
"Yes," replied the second convict, "kill me first."

A young couple were indulging in a spot of illicit passion in a dark secluded forest. After half an hour the young man got to his feet and said, "It's too dark here, I wish I had a torch."
To which his partner replied, "So do I, you've been eating grass for the last 30 minutes."

A chicken and an egg are lying side-by-side in bed. The chicken has a blissful look on his face and is smoking a cigarette. The egg looks at the chicken and says, "Well I guess you've answered that question then."

෴෴෴෴

What do Saddam Hussein and nylon knickers have in common?

They both irritate Bush

෴෴෴෴

How can you tell if your dog is kinky?

It starts having sex in the missionary position

———————

What's the difference between in-laws and outlaws?

Outlaws are wanted!

What do sex and money in the bank have in common?

If you take it out too soon you lose interest

৵৵৵৵

What is a man's idea of foreplay?

One hour of begging

Why don't boxers make love before a fight?

Because they don't fancy each other

Why don't gypsies use condoms?

They can see what's coming

_____

What is the world's biggest drawback?

An elephant's foreskin

৵৵৵৵

43

"The room is £45 a night. It's £15 if you make your own bed."

"I'll make my own bed."

"Good! I'll get you some nails and wood."

Mary had a little lamb that
ran into a pylon,
2000 volts shot up its bum and
turned its wool to nylon.

☙☙☙☙

What do you get if you cross a
Viagra tablet with a chocolate
biscuit?

A biscuit that stays hard when
you dip it in your tea

———————

What did one lesbian frog say
to the other?

Would you believe it, we really
do taste like chicken!

"Little Billy went to school and walked into the classroom with a huge lump under his pullover.

"What on earth have you got there?" asked the teacher.

Billy sheepishly lifted his pullover and his pet cat Tiddles shot across the classroom.

"Now tell me, Billy," scolded his teacher, "what possible reason could you have for bringing your cat into school?"

Billy replied, "As I was getting ready for school this morning, I heard the milkman saying to my mummy, as soon as young Billy gets off to school I'm going to eat your pussy."

A man walks into a bar and reads a sign ... FREE BEER FOR THE PERSON WHO CAN PASS THE TEST! So he asks the barman what the test is. The barman replies, "Well, first you have to drink that gallon of tequila, the WHOLE lot at once. Second, there's a crocodile out the back with a sore tooth ... you have to remove it with your bare hands. Third, there's a woman upstairs who's never had an orgasm. You gotta make things right for her." The guy thinks about it and quickly realises he'd have to be mad.

Well, as time goes on and the man drinks a few, he asks, "Where's that tequila?" He grabs the gallon of tequila with both hands, and downs it with a big slurp and tears streaming down his face. Next, he staggers out back and soon all the people inside hear the most frightening roaring and thumping, then silence. The man staggers into the bar, his shirt ripped and big scratches all over his body.

"Now," he says, "where's that woman with the sore tooth?"

Two drunks had just been thrown out of a bar and were walking down the street when they came across a dog, sitting on the curb, licking its balls. They stand there watching and after a while one of them says, "I sure wish I could do that!" The other one looks at him and says, "Well, I think I'd pet him first."

༃ ༃ ༃ ༃

A blonde walks into a doctor's surgery complaining of feeling sick in the morning. The doctor examined her before saying, "Congratulations, it appears that you're pregnant."
"Oh my God!" screams the blonde. "Are you sure it's mine?"

A man was drinking in a pub when he was approached by a old man who poked him in the ribs and said, "Last night your mother gave me a blow job." The younger man ignored the jibe. The older man poked him in the chest and said, "Last night I bonked your mother for two hours solid." The younger man once again ignored him. The older man poked him once more and said, "Last week I had your mother from behind over the kitchen table!" The younger man sighed and said, "Go home Dad, you're pissed again."

———————

Two nuns are driving down a country lane in Transylvania. Suddenly Count Dracula lands on the bonnet of their car, and bares his yellowed fangs at them. The first nun screams, "Sister Mary, show him your cross!" Sister Mary winds down the window of the car, sticks her head out of the window and yells, "Hey goofy, get the f**k off my car!"

A tortoise limped into a police station with a bloody nose and a cut over his left eye. "What happened to you?" enquired the desk sergeant. "I was walking home from the pub when I was mugged by two snails," said the tortoise. "Can you give me a description of them?" "I don't know," the tortoise said, "it all happened so fast."

Two dog owners are arguing about whose dog is smarter. First owner: My dog is so smart, every morning he waits for the paper boy and then he brings me the paper. Second owner: I know ... my dog told me.

How are a turtle and a blonde the same?

Once they're on their backs, they're both screwed

ॐ ॐ ॐ ॐ

A dog walks into a bar, jumps up on the stool and says to the bartender, "Hey barman, it's my birthday today. How about a free drink?"
The bartender turns, looks at the dog and nods his head.
"Sure pal, toilet's right down the hall."

A businessman enters a tavern, sits down at the bar, and orders a double martini on the rocks. After he finishes the drink, he peeks inside his shirt pocket, then orders the bartender to prepare another double martini. After he finishes that, he peeks inside his shirt pocket again and orders the bartender to bring another double martini. The bartender says, "Look, buddy, I'll bring ya' martinis all night long – but you gotta tell me why you look inside your shirt pocket before you order a refill." The customer replies, "I'm looking at a photo of my wife. When she starts to look good, I know it's time to go home."

A man walks into a bar with a newt on his shoulder. The barman looks at the creature and asks the man what he calls it.
"Tiny," replies the man.
"Why's that?" asks the bartender.
"Because he's my newt!"

Two drunks were walking along a railway track when one said to the other, "This is the longest flight of stairs I've ever walked on." The other replied, "It's not the length that bothers me, it's the height of the handrails."

ॐ ॐ ॐ ॐ

What do you call a man with a truck on his head?

Laurie

———————

How do you get a man to stop biting his nails?

Make him wear shoes

A man went to see his doctor and said "My grandfather died aged 45 and my father died aged 40. I'm worried that I'll die young too, could you suggest anything to help me live longer?"
The doctor replied, "Give up smoking, drinking and sex."
"Will that make me live longer?" asked the man.
"I don't know, but it will seem like an eternity."

Roger goes to see his boss. "We're doing some heavy house-cleaning at home tomorrow, and my wife needs me to help with the attic and the garage, moving and hauling stuff."
"We're short-handed, Roger," the boss replies. "I can't give you the day off."
"Thanks, boss," says Roger, "I knew I could count on you!"

A mushroom walks into a bar and orders a drink. The barman says, "We don't serve mushrooms here." The mushroom says, "Why not? I'm a fun guy!"

Two Eskimos sitting in a kayak were chilly, but when they lit a fire in the craft it sank – proving once and for all that you can't have your kayak and heat it, too.

❧ ❧ ❧ ❧

" Doctor, doctor, I've got a steering wheel in my boxer shorts and it's driving me nuts! "

51

A lady was walking to work when she saw a parrot on a perch in front of a pet store. The parrot said to her, "Hey lady, you are really ugly." Well, the lady was furious! She stormed past the store to her work.

On the way home she saw the same parrot and it said to her, "Hey lady, you are really ugly."

She was incredibly angry now. The next day, the same parrot again said to her, "Hey lady, you are really ugly."

The lady was so annoyed that she went into the store and said that she would sue the store and kill the bird. The store manager apologised profusely and promised he would make sure the parrot didn't say it again.

When the lady walked past the store that day after work the parrot called to her, "Hey lady." She paused and said, "Yes?" The bird said, "You know."

A blonde is driving when her car crashes and she is hurled through the windscreen. An ambulance arrives and the medics rush over to the girl who is on the floor screaming, "I'm blind! I'm blind!" One of the medics tries his best to comfort her and says, "How many fingers do I have up?" "Oh my god!" screams the blonde. "I'm paralysed!"

ॐॐॐॐ

A Brooklyn woman prepared her will and made her final requests. She told her priest she wanted to be cremated and her ashes scattered at Bloomingdales. "Why Bloomingdales?" asked the priest. "At least I'll know my daughters visit me twice a week."

On Christmas morning a policeman on horseback is sitting at traffic lights, and next to him is a kid on his brand new bike. The policeman says to the kid, "Nice bike you got there. Did Santa bring that to you?" The kid says, "Yeah." The policeman says, "Well, next year tell Santa to put a light on that bike." The policeman then proceeds to issue the kid a £20 bicycle safety violation ticket. The kid takes the ticket and before the policeman rides off says, "By the way, that's a nice horse you got there. Did Santa bring that to you?" Humouring the kid, the policeman says, "Yeah, he sure did." The kid says, "Well, next year tell Santa to put the dick underneath the horse, instead of on top."

ॐॐॐॐ

53

A blind man walks in to a department store with his guide dog on a leash. As usual, the store manager behind the customer service counter looks up, notices the customer is blind, and not wanting to stare, quickly looks away again. Out of the corner of his eye the manager sees the blind man start swinging the dog over his head with its lead. Shocked, the manager runs over and says, "Sir, is there a problem – is there anything I can help you with?" The blind man calmly replies "No thanks – I'm just browsing."

A guy sits down in a café and asks for the hot chilli.
The waitress tells him, "The guy next to you got the last bowl." He looks over and sees that the guy has finished his meal, but the chilli bowl is still full.
He asks, "Are you going to eat that?"
The other guy says, "No. Help yourself."
He takes it and starts to eat it. When he gets about half way down, his fork hits something. He looks down, sees a dead mouse and pukes the chilli back into the bowl.
The other guy turns and says, "That's about as far as I got, too."

How many men does it take to wallpaper a room?

About two – if they're thinly sliced

Police officials have announced that all the toilets were stolen in a recent burglary at Scotland Yard. The thief is still at large and the police have nothing to go on.

ঔঔঔঔ

Two nuns are enjoying an illicit cigarette in their convent. The first nun finishes her cigarette and then produces a condom from her pocket and places the cigarette butt inside it.

"Where did you get that from?" asks the second nun.

"From the chemist around the corner. I suggest you go and buy some. If Mother Superior finds out we've been smoking we'll be in big trouble."

The second nun pays a visit to the chemist and asks for a single condom. The chemist is taken aback and asks, "What size would you like?" To which the nun replies, "Big enough to fit twenty Camels."

> A man is driving through the country at 50 miles an hour when he sees a chicken gaining ground on him. He speeds up to 60 miles an hour and turns to see that the chicken is right behind him. As he reachs 80 miles an hour the chicken pulls out to overtake him. He watches the chicken speed by and notices that the bird has three legs. It begins to pull away but desperately the driver follows. He watches the chicken turn into a lane to a farmhouse where the chicken disappears through the door of a barn. He stops to search for the bird when he sees a farmer,
>
> "Did a three-legged chicken pass you?" the man asks.
>
> "Probably," says the farmer, "we've been breeding a variety of three-legged chickens for the past six months"
>
> "Why three-legged chickens?" asks the man
>
> The farmer explains, "I live with my wife and son, and all of us love chicken legs, so I decided to breed three-legged chicken so we could have a leg each at dinner."
>
> "What do they taste like?" asks the man.
>
> "Dunno," replied the farmer, "we've never managed to catch one of the little buggers!"

What do you call a man with a seagull on his head?

Cliff

ॐॐॐॐ

A husband returned home early from work one day to find his wife lying naked in bed.
He noticed a cigar in the ashtray on the nightstand.
The husband yelled, "Where in the hell did THAT come from?"
A voice under the bed said, "Havana."

―――――――

A dyslexic man walks into a bra ...

A young man walked into a fortune teller's booth to have his palm read. The fortune teller grabbed his hand and studied the lines intently before announcing, "I see that you have not had sex with a girl for over a year."
The young man replied, "Gosh, can you tell that from looking at my love line?"
"No," she replied "from all the blisters."

ॐॐॐॐ

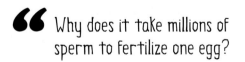 Why does it take millions of sperm to fertilize one egg?

They won't stop to ask for directions

William Shakespeare walked into his local, The Dog and Duck, leant on the bar and ordered a jar of the best house mead. The landlord eyed him with disdain and said, "Sod off you're Bard."

A man walked into a chemist's and said to the female counter assistant, "I would like six condoms please, Miss." "Don't you 'Miss' me!" retorted the assistant. "OK then, make it seven," replied the man.

ॐॐॐॐ

What's the best way to see flying saucers?

Trip up a waiter

——————

"Doc, I can't stop singing 'The green, green grass of home'." "That sounds like Tom Jones syndrome." "Is it common?" "It's not unusual!"

A guy walks into a bar and orders a drink. After a few more he needs to go to the toilet. He doesn't want anyone to steal his drink so he puts a sign on it saying, "I spat in this beer, do not drink!" After a few minutes he returns and there is another sign next to his beer saying, "So did I!"

——————

Two peanuts walk into a bar
One was a salted

A man walks into a bar with a giraffe and they proceed to get blitzed. The giraffe drinks so much it passes out on the floor. The man gets up and heads for the door to leave when the bartender yells, "Hey! You can't leave that lyin' there!" The drunk replies, "It's not a lion! It's a giraffe."

How does a man show he's planning for the future?

He buys two cases of beer instead of one

The Lone Ranger and Tonto were riding across the plains when Tonto heard a rumble in the distance. He leapt off his horse, put his ear to the ground, looked up at the Lone Ranger and said, "Buffalo come." "That's amazing!" said the Lone Ranger. "How can you tell that just by putting your ear to the ground?" "Face stuck," said Tonto.

ॐॐॐॐ

59

An accountant and a vicar are playing golf. On the first hole the accountant has a six-foot putt for par. He stroked the ball towards the hole and threw his club to the ground as it went by and shouted, "Bollocks, I missed!"

"Curb your language," said the vicar, "or God will send down a bolt of lightning and strike you dead."

At the next hole the accountant missed an easier putt and shouted, "Bollocks, I missed!"

"Curb your language," said the vicar, "or God will send down a bolt of lightning and strike you dead!"

At the tenth hole the accountant missed an even easier putt and screamed, "Bollocks, I missed!"

Suddenly a cloud opened and a flash of lightning sped down from the heavens and hit the vicar killing him stone dead. A voice boomed from up above, "Bollocks, I missed!"

Two pubic hairs are lying on their backs, stuck on the inside of a urinal in the men's toilets. The first pubic hair turns to the second and says, "Are you going to stay here much longer?" The second replied, "No, I think I'll just stick around for a while until I get pissed off."

৯৯৯৯

What's the definition of conceit?

Having an orgasm and calling out your own name

———————

An elephant walks into a pub and orders a drink. He was sipping his beer through his trunk when a man started to play the piano by his table. The elephant glanced over and began sobbing uncontrollably into his beer. "Why are you crying?" asked the barman. "Does this song have a special significance for you?" "No," wailed the elephant, "it's just that I think I recognize the keys."

———————

What's a blonde's favourite wine?

Daddy! I want a Porsche!

৯৯৯৯

Son: Where do I get all my intelligence from Dad?

Father: It must be your mother, I still have mine

A young businesswoman went into a sperm bank in the hope of receiving a donation to get pregnant. She was waiting in the doctor's surgery when the doctor walked into the room with his penis hanging out of his trousers.
"Doctor I have an appointment to collect a bottle of semen," said the woman, "but do you realize that your willy is hanging out of your trousers?"
"I know," replied the doctor, "we've run out of bottles, so you'll have to have draught."

A woman returned home from a shopping trip to find her husband hurtling around the house like a madman with a rolled up newspaper. "What on earth are you doing?" she asked.
"Killing flies," replied her husband. "I've got four so far, two males and two females."
"How can you tell male flies from female flies?" asked the wife.
"Easy," replied her husband. "The two males were on a beer can and the two females were on the phone."

————————

What do you call a chicken in a shell suit?

An egg

"Today, class, we are going to learn some new words. Can anyone give me a sentence with the word fascinate in it?" Little Bobby's hand shot up eagerly and the teacher said, "Go ahead, Bobby." Bobby puffed out his chest with pride and said, "My sister has a cardigan with twelve buttons on it, but she has such a big bust that she can only fasten eight."

How many ears did Davy Crockett have?

Three – his left ear, his right ear, and his wild front ear

You should always give 100% at work ...
12% Monday, 23% Tuesday, 40% Wednesday, 20% Thursday, 5% Friday

ॐ ॐ ॐ ॐ

 What do you get from a pampered cow?

Spoilt milk

Three blondes are undergoing a maths test. The examiner asks the first blonde, "What is 4 x 4?" To which the blonde replies, "36." He asks the second blonde, "What is 4 x 4?" to which she replies, "Saturday." Shaking his head he asks the third blonde, "What is 4 x 4?" The third blonde answers, "16." "Very good," said the examiner. "Now tell these other two how you reached that conclusion." "Easy," she said, "I just subtracted Saturday from 36."

ॐॐॐॐॐ

Grumpy was having a bath and feeling happy. Happy got out and got dressed.

"A wife arrived home one day to find her husband in bed with the next door neighbour. She ran downstairs, got a carving knife, ran back upstairs and dragged her husband out of the bed with the knife to his throat.

She led her husband downstairs and out into the back garden shed. She then placed his penis into a vice, tightening it as far as possible. She snapped the handle off the vice. "Please darling," screamed the husband, "you're not going to chop it off are you?" His wife handed him the knife and said, "No, you are." She then walked outside and set fire to the shed."

If a synchronised swimmer drowns, do the rest have to drown as well?

———————

A man walked into a pub and ordered a pint. He noticed that the pub was empty apart from one man alone at a table.
"I haven't seen him in here before" he said to the barman, "do you know who it is?"
"Yes," said the barman, "that's the famous painter Vincent Van Gogh."
Suitably impressed, the man approached Van Gogh and said, "I'm a great admirer of your work, can I get you a drink?"
"No thanks," replied Van Gogh, "I've got one ear."

"A koala bear went to visit a prostitute and using sign language the prostitute deduced that the bear would like to perform oral sex upon her. The pair got down to business and after ten minutes the koala bear stood up and put his coat on to leave. The prostitute stopped him and dragged him to the bookcase, grabbing a dictionary. She leafed through until she came to the word prostitute and pointed out the definition: Prostitute, a woman paid money for sexual favours. The koala bear flicked through the dictionary until he came to the word koala and pointed out the definition that read: Koala, bear that eats bush and leaves."

A burglar was ransacking the living room of a house when from the darkness a voice piped up, "Jesus is watching you." The burglar turned around, startled and peered into the darkness. Once more the voice said, "Jesus is watching you." This time the burglar noticed a parrot sat in the corner and approached it. As he walked up to the bird it said, "Jesus is watching you." Relieved that his activities had not been rumbled, he said to the parrot, "And what might your name be?" To which the parrot replied, "Abraham." "What kind of idiot calls a parrot Abraham?" chortled the burglar. "The same idiot that calls a Rottweiler Jesus," squawked the parrot.

ॐ ॐ ॐ ॐ

A man woke up dripping with sweat. "What's the matter darling?" asked his wife. Her husband replied, "I've just had a dream that I wrote the complete trilogy of *The Lord Of The Rings*." "Don't worry," said his wife "you've been Tolkien in your sleep again."

———————

I went to buy some camouflage trousers the other day but I couldn't find any

A youngster was enjoying himself at the swimming baths when the lifeguard grabbed him by the arm and roared, "Out you go young man, I am reporting you for peeing in the pool." "But everybody pees in the pool," protested the youngster. "Not from the diving board!" replied the lifeguard.

What do a blonde and your computer have in common?

You don't know how much either of them mean to you until they go down

ॐॐॐॐ

A husband returned home from work one day to find his wife running around the house clapping her hands gleefully and giggling like a schoolgirl.

"Why are you so happy?" asked the husband.

His wife replied, "I went to see the doctor today and after he examined me he told me that I had the breasts of an eighteen-year-old!"

Her husband snorted, "Did he not say anything about your fifty-year-old arse?"

"No," replied the wife, "your name never came up."

"

A crow was enjoying a leisurely stroll through a forest when he heard a cry for help in the distance. He followed the source of the cry and stumbled upon a huge hole in the ground with an elephant at the bottom.

"I fell down this hole and can't get out," said the elephant.

"Don't worry," said the crow, "I've parked my Porsche around the corner. I will attach a length of rope to the bumper and drag you out."

This the crow duly did and they went their separate ways. The next day the elephant was strolling through the forest and came upon the same hole. He was surprised to see the crow stuck at the bottom.

"Could you return the favour?" asked the crow. "My Porsche is parked around the corner."

"I can't drive, let me try something else," said the elephant.

The elephant straddled the hole and lowered his willy. The crow grabbed the elephant's member with his beak and was hauled to safety. The crow thanked the elephant and they both went their separate ways.

The moral of this tale is, if you have a dick like an elephant you don't need a Porsche to pull the birds.

"

Two jump leads walk into a bar. The barman says, "You guys better not start anything in here."

ঙ্কঙ্কঙ্কঙ্ক

There were two old men, one a retired professor of psychology and the other a retired professor of history. Their wives had talked them into a two-week stay at a hotel in the Lake District. They were sitting around on the porch of the hotel watching the sun set. The history professor said to the psychology professor, "Have you read Marx?" To which the professor of psychology said, "Yes, I think it's the wicker chairs."

An artist asked the gallery owner if there had been any interest in his paintings. "I've got good news and bad news," the owner replied. "The good news is that a gentleman enquired about your work and asked if it would appreciate in value after your death. When I told him it would, he bought all 15 of your paintings."
"That's wonderful!" the artist exclaimed. "What's the bad news?" With concern, the gallery owner replied, "He was your doctor."

ঙ্কঙ্কঙ্কঙ্ক

What do you call a nun with a washing machine on her head?

Sister Matic

"Doctor, I think that I'm a dog. I don't know what to do!" "A common canine complex," said the doctor. "Come over here and lie down on the couch." "Oh no, doctor. I'm not allowed on the furniture."

A guy runs into the pub and says, "Quick, pour me five shots of your best whiskey." The barman pours them and the man drinks them as fast as he can. "Wow, that's the fastest I've seen anyone drink," says the barman. "Well you'd drink that fast if you had what I had," the man says. "Oh my god." the bartender says, "What do you have?" The man replies "£1.20."

A lady walks into a chemist's and asks for some arsenic. The chemist asks, "What do you want with arsenic?" The lady says, "To kill my husband." "I can't sell you any for that reason," the chemist replies. The lady pulls out a photo of a man and a woman in a compromising position and shows it to the chemist. The photo shows her husband with the chemist's wife. He looks at the photo and says, "Oh, I didn't know you had a prescription!"

ॐ ॐ ॐ ॐ

My friend drowned in a bowl of muesli. A strong currant pulled him under.

A husband and wife were in their garden, when he noticed her expanding backside. He commented, "Boy, your ass is getting big – almost as big as the gas grill here." His wife angrily stomped across the garden, and he followed saying, "Yep, that thing is getting huge."
At this, the wife retreated to the far side of the garden. Soon he approached with a tape measure, acquired the width, and exclaimed, "It *is* as big as the gas grill!"
Later that night when they were in bed, the husband started making moves on his wife. She just turned away. "C'mon, honey," he said, "what's wrong?" She replied angrily "I'm not firing up this grill for just one little sausage!"

I went to the butcher's the other day and I bet him 50 quid that he couldn't reach the meat off the top shelf. And he said, "no, the steaks are too high!"

Where do you get virgin wool from?

Ugly sheep

What carries a sack and bites people?

Santa Jaws

ॐॐॐॐ

A man goes to a fancy dress party painted from head to toe in green paint with a woman strapped to his back. He's approached by the host of the party who asks, "What have you come as?"
"A teenage mutant ninja turtle," replies the green man.
"Why is that woman strapped to your back?" asks the host.
"Oh that's Michelle!" he replied.

———

"Mike was watching TV at home when his phone rang. "Hello, this is Dr Smith, we have your test results back."

"What do the results show?" asked Mike.

"I'm afraid you have a rare condition known as SLASH, which is a combination of syphilis, laryngitis, angina, shingles and herpes."

"Is it treatable?"

"Well, first we'll be changing your diet. You will be limited to pancakes and pizzas."

"Will that help to cure me?" Mike replied.

"No," replied the doctor, "but they're the only things that we can slide under the door!"

Quasimodo was cleaning the bell tower at Notre Dame when suddenly he came face to face with another hunchback. "Who are you?" asked Quasimodo.

"Who I am doesn't matter, what matters is that I aim to steal the heart of Esmerelda."

"Esmerelda belongs to me!" roared Quasimodo and ran towards his tormentor in a rage. The pair began fighting and Quasimodo was knocked to the ground. He sprang to his feet grabbing his assailant by the ankles and with great gusto swung him around his head, threw him across the room and saw him flying face first into the bells with a sickening yet melodic thud. He bounced off the bells and fell through the window to the ground below. A crowd gathered around the lifeless body and someone shouted, "Quasimodo is dead!" Quasimodo appeared through the massed throng shouting, "It is not I who is dead."

"Do you know this hunchback?" asked a Parisian law officer.

"No," said Quasimodo "but his face rings a bell."

Jesus walked into the Bethlehem job centre in search of work. The counter assistant said to him, "We have two jobs available. The first is a teaching job in Nazareth. That pays £500 a week, and the second is a banking job in Jerusalem which pays £1000 a week."
"I'll take the teaching job in Nazareth," said Jesus.
"May I ask why you want the teaching job when it's half the pay of the banking job?"
To which Jesus replied, "Because they hammer you with tax in Jerusalem."

ॐ ॐ ॐ ॐ

Why did the raspberry cry?

His parents were in a jam

A man walks into a pub and begins scrutinising with interest a sign above the bar that reads,

HAM SANDWICH £1.50
HAND JOB £5

He calls the barmaid over and says to her, "Are you the one giving hand jobs?"
"Yes," she said seductively.
To which the man replied, "Well go and wash your hands and make me a sandwich."

———

What's the difference between a blonde and a trampoline?

You take your shoes off before you jump on a trampoline!

Did you hear about the blind man who went bungee jumping?

He loved it, but it scared the hell out of his dog

A man walks into a bar, and orders a beer. As he sits there, the jar of nuts on the bar tells him what a nice shirt he is wearing. Disturbed by this, he goes to the cigarette vending machine to buy a pack of smokes. As he approaches the machine, it starts screaming and shouting at him. He runs to the bar and explains this to the barman. The barman apologizes and says, "The peanuts are complimentary, but the cigarette machine is out of order!"

Bob the milkman was doing his rounds when he was greeted at the front door by a busty blonde with a towel wrapped around her voluptuous curves. "Hello Bob," said the blonde, "I wonder if you can help me. I've always wanted to have a bath in milk." "Pasteurised?" asked Bob. "No, just up to my tits," said the blonde.

ॐॐॐॐ

Why are married women usually heavier than single women?

Single women come home, look at what's in the fridge and go to bed. Married women come home, look at what's in the bed and go to the fridge.

A lady went to see her gynaecologist who upon examining her proclaimed, "You have a very large vagina, you have a very large vagina, you have a very large vagina." "I know, but you didn't have to say it three times!" said the lady indignantly. "I didn't," said the gynaecologist.

What do wedding anniversaries and toilets have in common?

Men always miss them

What do you do if you come across a tiger in the jungle?

Wipe him clean, apologise and RUN!

_____

ॐ ॐ ॐ ॐ

What do you get if you pour boiling water down a rabbit hole?

Hot cross bunnies

_____

A blonde, a brunette and a redhead are drinking in a bar and boasting about their respective husbands. The blonde says, "I have the most generous husband in the world. Last week he booked a two-week holiday for us to Barbados and bought me a brand new Lamborghini!"

The brunette says, "I have the most intelligent husband in the world. He even has the letters BSc after his name which stand for Bachelor of Science!"

The redhead said, "I have the most well-endowed husband in the world. When his penis is erect twelve budgies can perch on it in single file!"

After a few more drinks the truth begins to come out.

The blonde says, "Actually I was exaggerating about my husband. Last week he booked a weekend in Blackpool and bought me a second hand Mini."

The brunette says, "I was exaggerating too. My husband is a builder and the BSc stands for Brick Sculptor."

The redhead says, "Actually I was exaggerating too. When my husband places the budgies on his erect penis the twelfth one has to stand on one leg."

A man is walking past a tiger's cage at the zoo when he notices a listless looking tiger lying on its side and casually licking its own bum. A zoo keeper walks past and the man grabs him and says, "This tiger is a bit of a let down, aren't they supposed to be fearsome creatures?"

"That is the fiercest tiger we have in the entire zoo," replies the zoo keeper.

"Then why is he just laying there licking his bum?" asked the man.

The zoo keeper replies, "Less than an hour ago that tiger escaped from its cage and ate a lawyer, bones and all."

"So, why is it licking its bum?" asks the man again.

"It's just trying to get the nasty taste out of its mouth," replies the zoo keeper.

A man went to see his doctor, complaining of a poor diet. "Tell me what you eat during the course of a day." The patient replied, "For breakfast I eat four red snooker balls and two yellow balls. For my lunch I have three brown snooker balls and six blue balls. For my dinner I have five pink balls and eight black balls. and sometimes I have two white cue balls for my supper."

The doctor thought for a moment then replied, "I think I know what your problem is, you're not getting enough greens."

What do you get if you offer a blonde a penny for her thoughts?

Change

A drunk was staggering home after a very heavy drinking session and a trip to his local curry house. No sooner had he digested his vindaloo when he felt a heaving in his stomach and proceeded to empty its entire contents over a passing cat. He looked down at the cat and remarked, "I don't remember eating that."

A man and a woman who've never met find themselves in the same sleeping carriage of a train. After a while, they both fall asleep – the woman on the top bunk, the man on the lower. In the middle of the night the woman leans over and says, "I'm sorry to bother you, but would you mind passing me another blanket?" The man leans out and with a glint in his eye says "I've got a better idea, let's pretend we're married." "Why not," giggles the woman. "Good," he replies. "Get your own blanket."

Why did the leper fail his driving test?

He left his foot on the clutch

৵৵৵৵

What's the difference between a supermarket trolley and a rugby player?

A trolley has a mind of its own

A man walked into the doctor's surgery and said, "Doctor, every time I break wind it sounds like a Honda motorbike."

"That's interesting, is there anything else bothering you?" asked the doctor.

"I also have a huge boil on my backside," said the man ruefully.

"Right," said the doctor, "I will lance the boil and all your problems will disappear."

"How's that?" asked the man.

To which the doctor replied, "Because abscess makes the farts go Honda."

A man walked into a pub and ordered ten double whiskies. He lined them up along the bar and proceeded to down each glass one after the other. "Celebrating or drowning your sorrows?" asked the barman. "My first blow job," said the man. "Congratulations," said the barman, "have one on me." "No thanks," the man replied, "if ten double whiskies doesn't take the taste away, nothing will."

ॐ ॐ ॐ ॐ

"Do you believe in life after death?" the boss asked Frank. "Yes, Sir," Frank replied. "That's good," the boss said. "After you left early to go to your grandmother's funeral, she stopped in to see you."

Patient: Doctor, doctor I think I'm a chicken. Doctor: How long have you felt this way? Patient: For over a year now. Doctor: Why did you wait this long before you came to see me? Patient: We needed the eggs!

———————

What should you give an elf who wants to be taller?

Elf-raising flour

What does a blonde put behind her ears to make her more attractive?

Her ankles

ॐ ॐ ॐ ॐ

An ice cream man was found lying on the floor of his van covered with hundreds and thousands. Police say he may have topped himself.

————————

A blonde walked into a sex shop and said, "Could I see your range of vibrators please?"

The assistant replied, "We have a black vibrator, 7 inches long, satisfaction guaranteed. We also have a red one, 8 inches long, satisfaction guaranteed. Our top of the range model is a purple one, 12 inches long, satisfaction guaranteed."

"What about that tartan one on the shelf?" asked the blonde.

"I'm afraid you can't buy that one," said the shop assistant, "that's my thermos flask."

Two Irishmen, Paddy and Seamus, are walking home from a night on the town when Paddy turns to Seamus and says, "Seamus, look, it's a long walk home, why don't we steal a bus?"

"Feck, that's a grand idea, Paddy. Tell you what, I'll nip into the bus depot and grab us a bus," replies Seamus.

"Sure Seamus," counters Paddy. So off trots Seamus to steal a bus. Paddy stands at the gates of the depot, watching. After 15 minutes he wonders were the feck Seamus has got to. He turns round to see Seamus running to one bus, looking in the window and then running on to the next.

"What the feck are you doing Seamus?" yells Paddy.

"Paddy, I cant find a route 109," shouts Seamus.

"You feckin' eejit," bellows Paddy, "just steal that 108 and we'll get off at the roundabout!"

A vacuum cleaner, a frying pan and a penis were chatting on a rubbish dump.

"I used to have the worst job in the world," said the vacuum cleaner. "Every day I had my tail plugged into a hole and was shoved around the house picking up dog hairs and dust."

"I can beat that," said the frying pan. "Every day I had hot oil poured into me, a fire lit underneath me and dead animals thrown on top of me!"

The penis looked at his two companions and said, "You had it easy. Every night I was suffocated with a plastic mac over my head and rammed into a dark hole until I threw up!"

ॐॐॐॐ

Joe manages to get a ticket to the FA Cup final, but on arriving he finds that it is right at the back of the top stand and has a pillar in the way of his view. So he starts looking around the stadium with his binoculars and sees a guy about five rows from the pitch on the halfway line with an empty seat beside him.

This is driving Joe nuts, so at half time, he goes down and asks the guy why he has a spare seat in such a great position.

The guy says, "My wife and I bought these seats a long time ago. But unfortunately, she passed away."

"Oh, I'm really sorry to hear that," Joe says.

"But why didn't you give the ticket to another relative or a friend?"

The guy replies, "They're all at the funeral."

85

A man walked into the doctor's with a black eye, a split lip and his arm in a sling.
"What happened to you?" asked the doctor.
"I was watching TV last night," said the patient "when there was a knock at the door.
I opened the front door to be greeted by a six-foot cockroach who head-butted me, punched me in the mouth and twisted my arm up my back."
"Yes," said the doctor, "there is a nasty bug going around."

How do men exercise on the beach?

By sucking in their stomachs every time they see a bikini

ॐॐॐॐ

A nun was enjoying a bath in the convent when there was a knock on the bathroom door.
"Who's there?" said the nun.
"It's the blind man," came the reply.
No harm in the blind man coming in thought the nun and said, "Enter my son."
The door opened and the man walked in and said, "Nice tits, Sister, where do you want these blinds?"

A woman was walking through a park when she noticed an old man sobbing uncontrollably. "Whatever is the matter?" she asked.
The old man looked up at her and through his tears wailed, "I am 80 years old and I am married to a six-foot tall, 21-year-old blonde. We make love in the morning, the afternoon and twice at night." "Then why are you crying?" asked the woman.
The old man dried his eyes and said ruefully, "Because I've forgotten where I live."

ॐ ॐ ॐ ॐ

A woman walks into a bar and asks for a double entendre ... so the barman gave her one!

A neutron goes into a bar and asks, "How much for a pint of lager?"

The bartender replies, "For you, no charge."

How many country and western singers does it take to change a light bulb?

Two – one to change the bulb and one to sing about the great times they had with the old bulb

———

What's the worst thing about oral sex?

The view!

A giraffe wanders into a pub and orders a pint of beer. He looks at the barman and said, "I wonder if you could help me. I'm looking for my brother. Have you seen him?"
"I don't know," replied the barman, "what does he look like?"

ॐॐॐॐ

A man walked into a pet shop, approached the counter and said to the assistant, "I would like to buy a fly please"
"Sorry sir," replied the assistant, "we sell hamsters, birds, goldfish, cats and dogs, but I'm afraid we don't sell flies."
"Well, you've got one in the window!" protested the man.

A guy walks into a bar, and sees a horse behind the bar serving drinks. The guy is staring at the horse, when the horse says, "Hey buddy. What are you staring at? Haven't you ever seen a horse serving drinks before?"
The guy says, "No, it's not that ... I just never thought the parrot would sell the place."

Did you hear about the Buddhist who refused his dentist's laughing gas?

He wanted to transcend dental medication

Why do men whistle whilst sitting on the toilet?

It helps them remember which end to wipe

A father and son walked into a chemist and the youngster skipped off towards the condom aisle and picked up a three-pack of condoms. "What are these for Dad?" asked the son innocently.

"They're for teenagers," said the father, "one for Friday, one for Saturday and one for Sunday."

The son then picked up a six-pack of condoms and said, "What are these for Dad?"

"They're for university students," said the father, "two for Friday, two for Saturday and two for Sunday."

The son then picked up a twelve-pack of condoms and said, "What are these for Dad?"

"They're for married men" said the father, "one for January, one for February ..."

A penguin was enjoying his driving holiday in the USA. The sun was shining and the penguin whistled a happy tune as he drove. His happiness soon turned to anger as smoke began to billow from his car's engine. As luck would have it, his car came to a halt right outside a mechanic's workshop. The penguin left the car and explained his problem to the mechanic.

"I'll see what I can do," said the mechanic, "but it will probably take a couple of hours."

"Are there any shops around here?" asked the penguin.

"Yes," replied the mechanic, "there's a supermarket one mile down the road."

The penguin left to walk to the supermarket. He walked through the doors and headed for the freezer department where he bought a tub of ice cream. He walked back to the workshop dipping his flipper into the tub and laughed as it smeared his face with ice cream. He finished eating and tossed the tub aside. On his arrival back at the workshop the mechanic greeted him and said, "It looks like you've blown a seal."

"No," said the penguin, "it's just ice cream."

There were three criminals who had just robbed a bank in Egypt. They were caught, convicted, and sentenced to exile in the Sahara Desert. They could each take only one thing with them. When they met in the desert they each asked what the others had brought.
"I brought a loaf of bread, so when I get hungry, I'll have something to eat," said the first criminal.
"I brought a water skin, so when I get thirsty, I'll have something to drink," said the second.
"I brought a car door, so that when it gets hot I can roll down the window."

"Doctor, doctor, I can't pronounce my Fs, Hs and Ts."

"Well you can't say fairer than that."

Jim and John were playing golf when a funeral procession drove past, as Jim was about to tee off. He stopped in mid-swing, put his golf club on the floor, removed his hat and bowed his head solemnly.
"Very touching," said John.
"It was the least I could do," said Jim, "after all I was married to her for 30 years."

ॐ ॐ ॐ ॐ

A man walked into a doctor's surgery and was greeted by a grim-faced doctor. "I'm afraid I have some bad news for you," said the doctor, "you have contracted cancer and you have only six months to live." "I knew it," replied the man and he began to sob uncontrollably "There's something else," said the doctor, "you also have Alzheimer's Disease." "Well, it could be worse," said the man, "at least I don't have cancer."

ॐ ॐ ॐ ॐ

Why do blondes have square breasts?

Because they forget to take the tissues out of the box!

Mable was driving Marge to the bingo. It was a sunny day with the radio playing, and the two of them quietly enjoyed their drive. Marge was shocked when Mable drove through a red light, but she didn't say anything. Then Marge gripped her seat, when Mable passed through a second red light. Marge thought she should say something, but didn't. She thought if Mable drives through another one, she will most certainly speak up. Sure enough, Mable drove through another red light. Marge screamed out, "Mable, what are you doing? That's the third red light you've driven through!" Mable replied, "I thought you were driving!"

_____

Two fish swim into a concrete wall. One turns to the other and says, "Dam!"

What do you call an intelligent blonde?

A golden retriever

ॐ ॐ ॐ ॐ

_____

A duck walked into a grocery store and asked, "Excuse me, do you have any fish?"

The shop assistant said, "No, duck, we don't have any fish." So the duck returned the next day to the same store and asked, "Excuse me, do you have any fish?"

The shop assistant replied, "No, I told you we don't have any fish and if you come back here again I'm going to staple your feet to the floor and call the police!"

So the duck came back again the next day to the same shop assistant and said, "Excuse me, do you have any staples?" The clerk said, "No, duck, we don't have any staples!"

So the duck says, "Then do you have any fish?"

What's the difference between
BSE and PMT?

One is mad cows' disease and the
other is an agricultural problem
that affects the livelihood
of farmers

Walking past the big wooden
fence around the insane
asylum, a guy hears everyone
inside chanting, "Thirteen!
Thirteen! Thirteen!"
His curiosity gets the better
of him so he finds a hole in
the fence and looks inside.
All of a sudden a finger shoots
through the hole, poking
him in the eye, and the
inmates start wildly chanting,
"Fourteen! Fourteen! Fourteen!"

**A man walking down the street
noticed a small boy trying to
reach the doorbell of a house.
Even when he jumped up, he
couldn't quite reach it. The
man decided to help the boy,
walked up on to the porch and
pushed the doorbell. He looked
down at the boy, smiled and
asked, "What now?"
The boy answered, "Now we
run like crazy!"**

———————

Why do women have orgasms?

It gives them an extra reason
to moan

ॐॐॐॐ

Why are women like condoms?

They spend 90% of their time in your wallet, and 10% on your dick

ॐॐॐ

When I was young I used to pray for a bike, then I realised that God doesn't work that way, so I stole a bike and prayed for forgiveness.

Why do men have difficulty making eye contact with women?

Because breasts don't have eyes

———————

How do you tell when a blonde has an orgasm?

She drops her nail file

An Australian named Frank was driving over Sydney Harbour Bridge when he noticed his girlfriend Debbie climbing up the side of the bridge. He stopped his car and shouted, "Debbie what are you doing for god's sake?"
"Frank, you've got me pregnant," she wailed.
"I'm going to end it all."
A tear welled in Frank's eye as he said, "You know Debbie, not only are you a wonderful shag, but you're a real sport too!"

A woman was standing in a crowded lift of the hotel she was staying in when a man got in and accidentally elbowed her in the breast. The man said, "I'm sorry! But if your heart is as soft as your breast, you'll forgive me." so the woman replies, "If your dick is as hard as your elbow then I'm staying in room 113."

༈ ༈ ༈ ༈

Why do blondes drive cars with sunroofs?

More leg room

———————

A lady went to see her psychiatrist, "I think I might be a nymphomaniac."
He says, "I'm sure I can help you. My fee is £100 an hour."
She replied, "How much for all night?"

༈ ༈ ༈ ༈

Where do you find a dog with no legs?

Right where you left him

How are husbands like lawn mowers?

They're hard to get started, they emit noxious odours, and half the time they don't work

A reporter was interviewing a 104-year-old woman: "And what do you think is the best thing about being 104?" She thought for a moment and said, "No peer pressure."

A guy walks into a pub with a dog under his arm, puts the dog on the bar and announces that the dog can talk and that he has £100 he's willing to bet anyone who says he can't. The barman takes the bet and the owner asks the dog, "What's the thing on top of this building which keeps the rain from coming inside?"
The dog answers, "ROOF." The barman says, "Who are you kidding? I'm not paying." The dog's owner says, "How about double or nothing and I'll ask him something else." The barman agrees and the owner turns to the dog and asks, "Who was the greatest baseball player of all time?" The dog answers with a muffled, "RUTH."
With that the barman picks them both up and throws them out the door. As they bounce on the pavement the dog looks at his owner and says, "DiMaggio?"

Ron and Don, two out-of-work actors were sitting in a pub when Ron announced, "I start a new acting job next week. I'm playing a pirate in a TV production of Treasure Island."

"Congratulations," said Don, "I'll see you the same time here next week." The following week Don arrived at the pub to see Ron sat at the table with a hook on his hand and a patch over his eye. "Are you still in character Ron?" he asked.

"No," he said, "I've actually lost my hand and my right eye."

"Good heavens!" exclaimed Don. "What on earth happened?"

Ron explained, "I was on the ship when I tripped over a cannonball and fell into the sea where a shark bit off my hand, so the director gave me a hook. The next day I was walking down the deck of the ship when a seagull crapped in my eye which I subsequently lost."

"You don't lose an eye from a seagull crapping in it!" said Don.

Ron replied, "You do if you forget you've got a hook!"

A family from a long line of prostitutes were sitting in their living room when the daughter asked, "Mother, when you were a prostitute how much did you charge for a blow job?"
The mother replied, "£20, but times were hard back then."
The little girl then said, "Grandmother when you were a prostitute how much did you charge for a blow job?"
The grandmother replied, "£10, but times were hard back then."
The little girl then said, "Great-grandmother when you were a prostitute how much did you charge for a blow job?"
The great-grandmother replied, "Nothing, but times were hard back then and we were just grateful for something warm to drink!"

Two Muffins were baking in an oven. One muffin turned to the other and said, "Damn, it's hot in here!" The other muffin said, "Holy Shit ... a talking muffin!"

———————

Bert took his Saint Bernard to the vet. "Doctor," he said sadly, "I'm afraid I'm going to have to ask you to cut off my dog's tail." The vet stepped back, "Bert, why should I do such a terrible thing?" "Because my mother-in-law's arriving tomorrow, and I don't want anything to make her think she's welcome."

ॐ ॐ ॐ ॐ

Why does the female praying mantis kill her mate after reproduction?

To stop the snoring before it starts

Jones sat in his lawyer's office. "Do you want the bad news first or the terrible news?" the lawyer said.
"Give me the bad news first."
"Your wife found a picture worth half a million dollars."
"That's the bad news?" asked Jones. "I can't wait to hear the terrible news."
"It's of you and your mistress."

ॐ ॐ ॐ ॐ

Two friends were standing in a bank when a pair of robbers came in. Not only did the thieves clean out the tills, but they walked around with bags and ordered everyone to throw their valuables in. Just as the robbers got to the pair, one of the friends turned to the other and said, "By the way, Joe, here's that twenty quid I owe you."

———————

"It's just too hot to wear clothes today," Jack said as he stepped out of the shower. "Honey, what do you think the neighbours would think if I mowed the lawn like this?"
"Probably that I married you for your money," she replied.

A rabbit managed to break free from the laboratory where he had been born and brought up. It wasn't long before he came to a hedge and, after squeezing under it, he saw a wonderful sight: lots of other rabbits, all free and nibbling the lush grass. "Hey," he called. "I'm a rabbit from the laboratory and I've just escaped. Are you wild rabbits?"

"Yes. Come and join us," they cried. He hopped over and started eating the grass. It tasted so good. "What else do you wild rabbits do?" he asked. "Well, you see that field there? It's got carrots growing in it. We dig them up and eat them." This he couldn't resist and he spent an hour eating the delicious carrots. Later, he asked them again, "What else do you do?"

One of the rabbits came close and spoke softly. "You see those rabbits," he said, pointing to the far corner of the field. "They're girls. We shag them. Go and try it." Well, our friend spent the rest of the morning screwing his heart out. He staggered back to the guys. "That was fantastic," he panted. "So are you going to live with us?" one of them asked. "I'm sorry, I had a great time but I can't." The wild rabbits stared at him, a bit surprised. "Why? We thought you liked it here."

"I do," our friend replied, "but I must get back to the laboratory. I'm dying for a cigarette."

"

The sole human survivor of a shipwreck is marooned on a desert island with a pig and a bull mastiff. A year passes and the man's sexual urges begin to get the better of him and to his horror he finds himself becoming more attracted to the pig. However his various attempts at a romantic liaison with the pig are thwarted by the mastiff, which begins to growl menacingly whenever he approached the pig. On numerous occasions he finds the pig alone and the moment he begins to undress, the mastiff always appears to spoil his fun. Two days later a ship sails by and the man lights a signal fire, but to his dismay the ship exploded into flames and sank to the bottom of the ocean. One hour later the man spots a young lady desperately trying to reach the shore and notices a fin approaching behind her. He wades into the water, beats off the shark with a piece of driftwood and drags the woman to safety.

"Thank you," she wails, "you've saved my life. If there is anything I can do for you, anything at all to repay you, I will gladly do it."

He looked earnestly at the woman as a sliver of salt water trickled down her cleavage and said, "Actually, there is one thing you could do for me. Do you think you could take the dog for a walk?"

"

A man and a woman were dining at a restaurant when quite suddenly all the colour drained from the man's face and he slid under the table. A passing waiter noticed this and said to the woman in a concerned voice, "Excuse me madam, but your husband has just slipped under the table." The lady replied, "No he hasn't, my husband has just walked into the restaurant."

৵৵৵৵

Two nuns are cycling down a village street when one turned to the other and says, "Sister Clarence, I don't think I've ever come this way before." "It must be the cobbles, Sister Theresa."

How many male chauvinists does it take to change a light bulb?

none, let the lazy cow cook in the dark

A man is walking down the street and he sees a boy riding a go-cart. The boy has his dog pulling it with a rope attached to the dogs balls. The man says "You know if you tied it around his neck, it would go much faster." The boy replies, "I know, but then I wouldn't get the cool siren!"

How many politicians does it take to change a light bulb?

Two – one to change it and one to change it back again

ॐॐॐॐ

A man walked into a pub and sat a monkey up on the bar. The monkey took a peanut from a bowl and inserted it into his backside before removing it and popping it into his mouth. "That's disgusting!" said the barman. "Disgusting, but practical," said the man with the monkey. "Last week we were in a snooker hall and he ate one of the balls. Since then he's checked the size of everything he eats."

A husband and wife were attending a cattle auction when a bull caught the eye of the wife. She approached the farmer accompanying the bull and said, "Is this bull virile?" "Virile," said the farmer, "why last year he mated 400 times!" Impressed the wife returned to her husband and said to him, "You could learn a thing or two from that bull, the farmer informs me that it mated 400 times last year." The husband looked at his wife and said, "Why don't you go back and ask the farmer if it mated 400 times with the same cow."

A man walked into a bar and the barman was a little perplexed at his appearance, as he had a huge muscular body, but his head was no bigger than an orange.

"I hope you don't mind me asking," said the barman, "but your head seems to be a little out of proportion to the rest of your body."

"It's a long story," said the man ruefully. "One day I was jogging along the beach when I heard a cry for help. I ran towards the sound and found a beautiful woman trapped under a rock. The woman informed me that she was the magic mermaid and would grant me one wish if I could free her from the rock. Without further ado I picked up the rock and tossed it into the sea and waited for my wish to be granted. She was the most beautiful woman I had ever set eyes on and I told her that my wish was to make love to her. However she told me that was the only wish she could not grant as being a mermaid she was a fish from the waist down. So I said to her, how about a little head then?"

The Lone Ranger and Tonto arrived in town and made their way to the nearest saloon, where they were greeted by a huge sign on the saloon door reading, NO RED INDIANS. The Lone Ranger turned to Tonto and said, "Sorry but you'll have to wait outside while I go in for a drink."

"But it's freezing!" complained Tonto.

"I won't be long," said the Lone Ranger as he tethered his horse Silver to a post. "Try jogging up and down the street. That'll keep you warm."

Ten minutes later the Lone Ranger is enjoying his second glass of whisky when a cowboy walks into the saloon and shouts, "Anybody in here got a white horse?"

"That would be me" said the Lone Ranger.

"Well you've left your injun running," said the cowboy.

Patient: Doctor, I keep painting myself gold.

Doctor: Don't be alarmed it's just a gilt complex.

ॐ ॐ ॐ ॐ

A man walked into a barber's shop with three hairs on his head, "What can I do for you today?" asked the barber.
"Comb my hair to the left," the man said.
"Oh no," said the barber, "one of your hairs has just fallen out."
"Comb them to the right then," said the customer.
The barber duly obliged before proclaiming, "I'm sorry sir but another hair has just fallen out."
"Oh, sod it," said the customer, "leave it messy!"

A teenager walked into a chemists and asked for a packet of condoms. "Hot date tonight?" enquired the chemist. "Yes," replied the youth, "I'm having dinner with my girlfriend's parents for the first time and afterwards she has promised me a night of passion beyond my wildest dreams." Six hours later he arrived at his girlfriend's home and was introduced to the parents. They are about to start dinner when the youth said, "Do you mind if I say grace?" His girlfriend whispered in his ear, "You didn't tell me you were religious." Her boyfriend whispered back, "You didn't tell me your father was a chemist."

ॐ ॐ ॐ ॐ

Which four animals does a woman like to have in her house?

A tiger in bed, a mink in her wardrobe, a jaguar in her garage and a jackass to pay for it all.

A pub manager is interviewing three women for a job and asks all three the same question. The question is, if you found a pound coin on the floor what would you do with it: The first applicant says she would put the pound coin into the till. The second says she would put it into the charity box on the bar. The third says she would put it into the tip box. Question – Which of the three applicants got the job? Answer – The one with the biggest tits.

After dying in a car crash, three friends go to Heaven for orientation. They are all asked the same question, "When you're lying in your casket, and friends and family are mourning over you, what would you like to hear them say about you?" The first guy immediately responds, "I would like to hear them say that I was one of the great doctors of my time, and a caring family man." The second guy says, "I would like to hear that I was a wonderful husband and school teacher who made a huge difference in the children of tomorrow." The last guy thinks for a moment, and then replies, "I guess I'd like to hear them say, 'Look, he's moving!'"

What do Star Trek and toilet paper have in common?

They both circle Uranus looking for Black Holes

☙☙☙☙

A woman walks up to a guy in a blue bathing suit and says, "Did you know your eyes match your trunks?" He says, "Why? Are my eyes bulging?"

A man takes his Rottweiler to see the vet. "My dog's cross-eyed, is there anything you can do for him?" "Well," says the vet, "let's have a look at him." So he picks the dog up and examines his eyes, then checks his teeth. Finally, he says, "I'm going to have to put him down." "What? Because he's cross-eyed?" "No, because he's really heavy."

A man walks into the doctor's office. "What seems to be the problem?" asks the doc. "I have five penises." replies the man "Blimey!" says the doctor, "How do your trousers fit?" "Like a glove."

Sister Mary burst into Father Thomas's office in a state of agitation. "Father!" she cried, "just wait until you hear this!" The priest led the sister to a chair, and said, "Calm down and tell me what has you so excited?"

"Well, father," the nun began, "I was just walking to the chapel and I heard some of the boys wagering money!"

"A serious infraction, indeed!" said the priest.

"But that's not what has me so excited, father," she replied "it was WHAT they were wagering ON! They had wagered to see who could urinate the highest on the wall!"

"What an incredible wager! What did you do?"

"Well, I hit the ceiling, father."

"How much did you win?"

Two little boys, Sammy and Tim, were sharing a hospital room. As they were getting to know each other, Sammy asked Tim, "Hey Tim, what are you in for?"

"I'm having my tonsils out, I'm a bit worried," said Tim.

"I had my tonsils out and it was great! I got to eat all the ice cream I wanted for two weeks!"

"Oh yeah?" replied Tim. "That's not half-bad. Hey, Sammy, how about you? What're you here for?"

"I'm having a circumcision," Sammy answered.

"Oh my god, circumcision. I had one of those when I was a baby and I couldn't walk for two years!"

A drunk was staggering down the street when he wandered into a church. He bounced down the aisle, banging his legs on the pews before reeling into the confessional box. He sat down and after a couple of minutes heard a voice saying, "Can I help you my son?" "Sure can," slurred the drunk. "Do you think you could pass me some toilet paper?"

❧❧❧❧

What do you do if an elephant comes through your window?

Swim!

_____

A buxom woman walked into the doctor's surgery. The doctor was immediately attracted to her and began to squeeze her knee. "Do you know why I'm doing this?" asked the doctor.

"Checking for housemaids knee?" replied the woman

"That's right," said the doctor and began to caress her breasts. "What am I doing now?" said the doctor. "Checking for lumps?"

"That's right," said the doctor and removed all of his clothes and began to make love to the woman.

"What am I doing now?" asked the doctor.

"Catching syphilis," said the woman, "that's why I'm here."

Why are hurricanes named
after women?

Because they make a lot of noise
when they're coming and when
they leave they take half of your
house with them.

What does an accountant use for
birth control?

His personality

_____

**First cow: What do you think
of this mad cow's disease?**

**Second cow: Don't ask me,
I'm a duck!**

Sometimes I wake up grumpy
and sometimes I let her sleep

_____

**A man took part in a
newspaper's best pun
competition, entering ten
different puns in the hope that
at least one would win a prize.
Unfortunately no pun
in ten did!**

ཉ་ཉ་ཉ་ཉ་

What's the difference between
a lawyer and a bucket of
horse manure?

The bucket

What has four wheels and flies?

A dustbin lorry

ঔ ঔ ঔ ঔ

First snake: Are we poisonous?

Second snake: No, why?

First snake: I've just bitten my tongue

What do women's breasts and toy cars have in common?

Both were designed for children but dads end up playing with both

Why did the chicken cross the football pitch?

Because it heard the referee was blowing fouls

———

" A neutron walks into a pub and asks, "How much for a pint of beer?" The barman replies, "For you, no charge." "

A woman walked up to an old man sitting in a chair on his porch. "I couldn't help but notice how happy you look," she said. "What's your secret for a long, happy life?"
"I smoke three packs a day, drink a case of lager, eat fatty foods, and never, ever exercise," he replied.
"Wow, that's amazing," she said, "How old are you?"
"Twenty-six."

———————

If a drummer and a bass guitarist caught a taxi, which one would be the musician?

The taxi driver

"A man was riding in his limo when he noticed two men eating grass. He ordered his driver to stop and got out. "Why are you eating grass?" he asked. "We don't have any money for food," the man replied. "Come with me then." the man said excitedly. "But sir, I have a wife and two children!" "Bring them along! And you come too," he said to the other man. "But, I have a wife and six children!" the second man said. "Bring them as well." So, they climbed into the car. "You are too kind. Thank you for taking all of us with you." The rich man replied, "No, thank you ... the grass at my place is about 3-feet-tall and I could use the help!"

The class homework was to write about something unusual that happened during the past week. Little Timmy got up to read his. "Daddy fell in the well last week," he began.
"Good heavens," shrieked Mrs Johnson, the teacher. "Is he all right now?" "He must be," said Timmy. "He stopped yelling for help yesterday."

ॐ ॐ ॐ ॐ

Why did the leper go back into the shower?

He forgot his Head and Shoulders

A man in a bar had one too many drinks. A beautiful lady sat down next to him. He turned to her and said "Hey, how about it? You and me, getting it on. I've got a couple of quid and it looks like you could use a little money." She stands up and says, "What makes you think I charge by the inch."

What do you get if you cross a Jehovah's Witness and a punk?

Someone who knocks at your door and tells you to f**k off

ॐ ॐ ॐ ॐ

The streets were lined with mourners as a funeral procession drove slowly by. The convoy of vehicles drove slowly up the steep hill heading for the cemetery. As it reached the top of the hill, a cat ran in front of the lead car, causing the driver to slam on his brakes. The doors of the hearse flew open and the coffin spilled out onto the road. Due to the steepness of the hill it began to slide downwards, picking up speed. It sped by the pub and continued down towards the town centre. The coffin hurtled through the bus terminal and headed towards the shopping centre, scattering shoppers in its wake.

Through the shopping centre it sped and appeared to be heading to a crashing halt as it approached a pair of glass doors at the chemists. But the automatic doors opened and it slid through them and down the main aisle, scattering toiletries all over. It approached the main counter, and as it passed the lid slowly opened and its presumed dead occupant slowly sat upright and said to the startled pharmacist, "Have you got anything to stop this coffin?"

Wife: Give me some money.
I want to buy a bra.
Husband: What for? You've
got nothing to put in it!
Wife: Well, you wear shorts!

A vicar, known for his lengthy services, noticed a man get up and leave during the middle of his message. The man returned just before the end of the service. Afterwards the vicar asked where he had gone. "I went to get a haircut." "But, why didn't you do that before the service?" the vicar asked. "Because," the gentleman said, "I didn't need one then!"

ॐ ॐ ॐ ॐ

A man arrived in hell to be greeted by Satan who led the man down a corridor. There were three doors and the devil said, "You may choose one of these rooms to reside in." The devil opened the first, to reveal a man hanging by his thumbs whilst a goblin stabbed him with a poker. The man shook his head and the devil lead him to the second door. The door opened to reveal a man tied to a rock with rats chewing at his feet. The man shook his head again and the devil motioned him towards the final door. The door opened to reveal an old man chained to the wall. A beautiful blonde was knelt down giving the man a blow job. The new arrival smiled and nodded eagerly. Satan turned and said, "Debbie, your replacement's arrived."

A young man was forced to take a day off from work to appear for a minor traffic offence. He grew increasingly restless as he waited hour after endless hour for his case to be heard. When his name was called late in the afternoon, he stood before the judge, only to hear that court would be adjourned for the rest of the afternoon and that he would have to return the next day.

"What for!" he snapped at the judge. His honour, equally irked by a tedious day and sharp query, roared out loud, "£20 for contempt of court! That's why!" As the young man reached for his wallet, the judge relented, "That's all right. You don't have to pay now." The young man replied, "I know. I'm just checking to see if I have enough for two more words."

A young businessman had just started his own firm. He'd rented a beautiful office and had it furnished with antiques. Sitting there, he saw a man come into the outer office. Wishing to appear busy, the businessman picked up the phone and started to pretend he had a big deal in progress. He threw huge figures around and made giant commitments. Finally, he hung up and asked the visitor, "Can I help you?" The man said, "Sure. I've come to install the phone!"

Bob and Earl were huge baseball fans. Their entire lives, they discussed baseball history in the winter, and they pored over every score during the season. They went to 60 games a year. They even agreed that whoever died first would try to come back and tell the other if there was baseball in heaven.

One summer night, Bob passed away in his sleep after watching the Yankees' victory earlier in the evening. He died happy. A few nights later, his buddy Earl awoke to the sound of Bob's voice from beyond. "Bob is that you?" Earl asked. "Of course it's me," Bob replied.

"This is unbelievable!" Earl exclaimed. "So tell me, is there baseball in heaven?"

"Well I have some good news and some bad news for you. Which do you want to hear first?"

Earl excitedly replied, "Tell me the good news first."

"Well, the good news is that yes, there is baseball in heaven, Earl."

"Oh, that's wonderful! So what could possibly be the bad news?"

"You're pitching tomorrow night."

"

A man was dining in a fancy restaurant and there was a gorgeous redhead sitting at the next table. He had been checking her out since he sat down, but lacked the nerve to talk to her. Suddenly, she sneezed and her glass eye came flying out of its socket towards the man. He instantly reached out, grabbed it out of the air, and handed it back. "Oh my, I am so sorry," the woman said as she popped her eye back in place. "Let me buy you dinner to make it up to you." They enjoyed a wonderful dinner together, and afterwards the theatre followed by drinks. They talked, they laughed, she shared her deepest dreams and he shared his. After paying for everything, she asked him if he would like to come to her place for a night-cap ... and stay for breakfast. The next morning, she cooked a gourmet meal with all the trimmings. The guy was amazed! Everything had been so incredible! "You know," he said, "you are the perfect woman. Are you this nice to every guy you meet?"

"No," she replied, "you just happened to catch my eye."

"

A ventriloquist at a club is littering his act with dumb blonde jokes. Halfway through his routine a blonde jumps to her feet and declares, "I'm sick and tired of comedians like you telling blonde jokes. We are not all completely stupid."

"Calm down" said the ventriloquist. "It's only a bit of fun!"

"I'm not talking to you," screamed back the blonde, "I'm talking to that lippy bugger sat on your knee."

ॐ ॐ ॐ ॐ

What's the difference between a lawyer and an onion?

No one cries when you chop up a lawyer

Adam was walking through the Garden of Eden when God appeared before him. "What's the matter Adam, you're looking a little glum," said God. "I'm lonely," said Adam, "and need a companion."

"I can create you a companion," said God. "I will call the companion woman, she will cook for you without complaint, clean the garden without complaint and iron your fig leaf without complaint. She will give you untold pleasure whenever you desire it, nurse you when you are ill and fulfil your every whim throughout the day and night."

"She sounds wonderful," said Adam, "how much will this woman cost?"

"An arm and a leg," said God. "That's a bit expensive!" said Adam. "What can I get for a rib?"

A teacher was giving a sex education lesson at school and drew a penis on the blackboard. "Does anyone know what this is?" asked the teacher. Little Jimmy put his hand up and said, "That's a penis, Miss, and my daddy has two of them."
The startled teacher replied, "No Jimmy, you must be mistaken. Men only have one."
"No, my daddy has two," insisted Jimmy, "a small wrinkly one when he goes to the bathroom and a long hard one for brushing the babysitter's teeth."

———————

I went to a seafood disco last week ... and pulled a mussel.

ॐ ॐ ॐ ॐ

A man went to see the doctor with a carrot in his left nostril, a parsnip in his right nostril, a banana in his left ear and a leek in his right ear.
"I'm not feeling very well!" he informed the doctor.
"I can see what your problem is," replied the doctor, "you're not eating properly."

What's the difference between a female lawyer and a Doberman?

Jewellery

What do you do if a bird shits on your car?

Don't ask her out again

ॐ ॐ ॐ ॐ

A man walks into a bar and notices a group of people playing poker at a nearby table. To his amazement included in the group is a large Alsatian studying his hand intently. The man leans over to the bartender and asks, "Is that dog really playing poker?"

"He certainly is Sir," replied the bartender

"I find that utterly unbelievable," said the man.

"No, it's true. Every night the same group come in here with that dog and spend the evening playing poker."

"Is the dog any good?" asked the man.

"No, he's bloody rubbish!" came the reply. "Every time he gets a good hand his tail starts wagging."

A group of Hollywood moguls decided to make a film chronicling the history of classical music. They approached Jack Nicholson and told him that if he would star in their film he could play the composer of his choice. "I will play Mozart," said Nicholson. "Just like me he was known for being zany and having a wild streak." The moguls pleased with their coup at signing Nicholson then approached Tom Hanks who informed them that he was a huge fan of Beethoven and had always wanted to play him on film. Finally the moguls approached Arnold Schwarzenegger telling him of their project and asked him which composer he would like to play. "I'll be Bach," said Arnie.

A man walked into a tattoo parlour, "I would like £1000 tattooing along the length of my penis," said the man. The tattooist obliged and when he had finished his handiwork said, "I hope you don't mind me asking but this is a very unusual request. Could you tell me why you want a £1000 tattoo on your willy?" "Three reasons" said the man, "I like to play with money, I like to watch money grow and yesterday my wife said that she'd love to blow £1000."

———————

What is a blonde's definition of safe sex?

Shutting the car door

**How do you get an old lady
to swear?**

**Get another old lady to shout
Bingo!**

 App App App

"Waiter! This coffee tastes
like mud."
"Yes sir, it's fresh ground."

A magician was at home with his wife and two children when he began to practise some tricks. He strode around the lounge waving his wand when suddenly there was a flash of lightning and his wife turned into a couch whilst his children turned into a pair of armchairs. He waved his wand attempting to reverse the spell, but to no avail. In desperation he rang 999 and an ambulance soon arrived to transport his wife and children to hospital. Later the magician rang the hospital. "Hello," he said, "my name is Marvo the Magician. I accidentally turned my wife and children into a couch and two armchairs. Could you tell me how they are?" The voice at the other end of the phone replied, "Don't worry Sir, they're comfortable"

Did you know that Percy Shaw was inspired to invent cat's eyes when he saw a cat walking towards him down the middle of a road? This begs the question, if the cat had been walking away from him, would he have invented the pencil sharpener?

Why did the Avon lady get pregnant?

Because Max Factor

_____

What do you get when a leper takes a bath?

Soup

ॐ ॐ ॐ ॐ

A young lady entered a chemist's shortly after eating a salad sandwich for her lunch. She walked up to the counter and said to the chemist, "A packet of face wipes please." The slightly deaf chemist assistant replied, "Come again?" "No," replied the young lady, "mayonnaise."

Why do husbands usually die before their wives?

Because they want to

ॐ ॐ ॐ ॐ

Why did the nurse give the 85-year-old patient a Viagra?

To stop him rolling out of bed

ॐ ॐ ॐ ॐ

What's the difference between snowmen and snowwomen?

Snowballs

What's the difference between erotic and kinky?

Erotic is using a feather during sex, kinky is using the whole chicken

What's green and smells of pork?

Kermit's finger

" Did you hear about the dyslexic, agnostic, insomniac? He stayed awake all night wondering if there was a dog! **"**

Why do all men want to marry
a virgin?

Because they can't stand
criticism

Why did God create man?

**Because vibrators can't mow
the lawn.**

**A guy was reading his paper
when his wife walked up
behind him and smacked him
on the back of the head with
a frying pan. He asked,
"What was that for?"
She said, "I found a piece of
paper in your pocket with
'Betty Sue' written on it."
He said, "Honey, remember
last week when I went to the
races? 'Betty Sue' was the
name of the horse I went
there to bet on." She shrugged
and walked away. Three days
later he was reading his paper
when she walked up behind
him and smacked him on the
head with the frying pan again.
He asked "What was that for?"
She replied, "Your horse
called."**

ॐ ॐ ॐ ॐ

A man walked into a tool shop and said to the assistant, "Could I have a box of nails please?"
"How long would you like them?" inquired the assistant
"Forever," replied the man.

How do you make five pounds of fat more attractive?

Put a nipple on it

࿐ ࿐ ࿐ ࿐

What did the zero say to the eight?

Nice belt

The Lone Ranger and Tonto climbed off their horses outside a saloon. Tonto watched in amazement as the Lone Ranger lifted his horse's tail and planted a kiss on it's bum.

"Why did you kiss Silver's rear end?" asked Tonto.

"Chapped lips," replied the masked hero.

"Does that cure it?" asked Tonto.

"No," replied the Lone Ranger, "but it stops me from licking them."

"

Cinderella had reached the age of 90. Prince Charming had died long ago and her only companion was her cat, Bob. One day she was sitting in her rocking chair when her fairy godmother suddenly appeared. "Hello Cinderella," said the fairy, "how nice to see you."

"Hello," said Cinderella, "it's lovely to see you, but what brings you here?" "I am proud of the life you've led. I've decided to grant you two more wishes!" said the fairy. Cinderella thought long and hard before saying, "My first wish is to have the body of a young woman again."

The fairy godmother waved her wand and Cinderella turned into the beautiful young woman she once was. "And what is your second wish?" Cinderella thought long and hard before saying, "I would like you to turn my cat Bob into a handsome prince." The fairy godmother waved her wand and Bob the cat was transformed into a muscular Adonis with long flowing hair. "Goodbye," said the fairy godmother, "I will leave you now."

Cinderella walked over to Bob and he grabbed her in his arms and tenderly kissed her on the cheek. As he drew her closer to him he nibbled on her earlobe and whispered softly in her ear, "I bet you regret having me neutered now, don't you?"

"

A woman was rummaging through the freezers at a supermarket attempting to find a turkey large enough to feed her family of ten. "Do these turkeys get any bigger?" she enquired of a passing blonde store assistant.
"No madam," said the blonde, "they're dead."

જ્જ્જ્જ્

God was chatting to St Peter when he boomed, "I have just created a time period of 24 hours, part of which is illuminated by the Sun and part of which is covered in darkness!"
"And what are you going to do now?" asked St Peter.
God replied, "I think I'll call it a day."

A blonde walked into a doctor's surgery and said, "Doctor I hurt all over from my head to my toe."
"Show me exactly where it hurts," said the doctor. The blonde touched her elbow and said, "That really hurts," then touched her ankle and said, "that really hurts," then touched her chin and said, "that really hurts."
"I think I know what the problem is," said the doctor, "you've broken your finger."

——————

What type of food reduces a woman's sex drive by 80%?

Wedding cake

જ્જ્જ્જ્

131

A middle-aged woman placed an advert in the lonely hearts column in her local newspaper that read, **HUSBAND WANTED** Two days later she got out of bed to be greeted by a mass of letters, all of which were replies to her advert. Out of the 100 replies she received 96 of them read, **YOU CAN HAVE MINE**

ॐॐॐॐ

How do you make a blonde's eyes sparkle?

Shine a torch in her ear

———————

When do women care for a man's company?

When he owns it

ॐॐॐॐ

How many premenstrual women does it take to change a light bulb?

ONE FOR GOD'S SAKE!

Why can't blondes count to 70?

Because 69 is a bit of a mouthful

What's a guy that hangs out with musicians called?

A drummer

ॐॐॐॐ

A newly-wed wife and husband are discussing their past marriages. "As you know, I was married three times previously but I never had sexual intercourse with any of my husbands!" said the wife.

"I knew you'd been married three times," said the husband, "but I can't believe that you didn't have sex with any of them."

"It's true," said the wife. "My first husband was a psychiatrist and all he wanted to do was talk about it. My second husband was a gynaecologist and all he wanted to do was look at it. My third husband was a stamp collector, and I do miss him!"

A new police officer was assigned to ride in a car with a more experienced partner. A call came over the car's radio telling them to disperse some people in town who were loitering. The officers drove to the street and immediately observed a small crowd standing on one corner.

The rookie rolled down his window and said, "Let's move off the corner." No one moved, so he barked again, "Let's move off the corner, now!" Intimidated, the group of people began to leave, casting puzzled glances in his direction. Proud of his first official act, the young policeman turned to his partner and asked, "Well, how did I do?"

"Pretty good," said the veteran, "considering this is a bus stop."

ॐ ॐ ॐ ॐ

One day there were three moles at the breakfast table. Mama Mole came out and said, "I smell sugar and sweet things." Then Papa Mole stuck his head out the hole to get some fresh air and said, "I smell sour." Then Baby Mole came and stuck his head out the window, "I smell mole-asses."

Three Chinese men called Hu, Chu and Fu emigrated to the United States. On their arrival they applied for American citizenship and each of them decided to give their names a more American flavour. Hu changed his name to Huck, Chu changed his name to Chuck and Fu changed his mind and went back to China.

A hedgehog scurried into a pub, leant against the bar and said, "A pint of your finest beer please, landlord." "We don't serve hedgehogs in here," replied the landlord "That's OK," replied the hedgehog, "I don't eat them."

A teenager walked into the doctors and said, "Doctor, I'm having the strangest recurring dreams."

"Describe these dreams," said the doctor.

The teenager replied, "On Monday night I dreamt I was on stage, singing 'Love Is All Around' in front of hordes of screaming girls. Last night I dreamt I was on stage singing 'Wishing I Was Lucky' in front of hordes of screaming girls."

"Don't worry," said the doctor, "this is quite common for boys of your age. They're just wet, wet, wet dreams."

A man goes to a fancy dress party dressed only in his Y-fronts. A woman comes up to him and asks "What are you supposed to be?" The man says "A premature ejaculation." "What?" says the woman. The man says, "I've just come in my pants."

Why did the koala fall out of the tree?

Because it was dead

Did you hear about the flasher who was considering retirement but decided to stick it out for another year?

Sharon was walking through the town centre one day when she noticed her friend Carole the blonde, dragging a door behind her. "Why are you dragging a door around?" asked Sharon. Carole grimaced and replied, "Because I've lost my front door key."
"What are you going to do if you lose your front door?" joked Sharon.
"I'm not stupid you know," replied Carole, "I've left the kitchen window open."

Did you hear about the village idiot who put a condom on backwards and went?

What should you do if your girlfriend starts smoking?

Use a lubricant

A man and his wife are driving down the road when a policeman pulls them over. The policeman says to the man, "Do you know that you were speeding?" The man replies, "No sir, I didn't know I was speeding." The man's wife yells, "Yes you did, you knew you were speeding I've been telling you to slow down for miles!"

"SHUT UP!" the man says to his wife, "Shut the hell up, just sit back and be quiet." Then the policeman says, "Well, since I've got you pulled over did you know that your left rear brake light isn't working?"
"No Sir," the man replies, "I didn't know that."

"You liar!" his wife yells. "I've been telling you to get it fixed for two months now!" "Shut up!" the man yells at his wife again. "Sit back and shut up, mind your own business!" Curious, the policeman walks over to the woman's side of the car and asks her, "Does he always talk to you this way?" "No," she replies, "only when he's drunk!"

It is the tenth Animal Jungle Olympics. In the previous nine games the 800 metres had been dominated by Larry the leopard, but this year Larry decided that he needed a new challenge. He approached the organiser of the games, Edward the elephant, and said, "Edward, this year I wish to compete in the pole vault as I'm getting bored with the ease in which I win the 800 metres." Edward looked at Larry and shook his head before saying, "Sorry Larry, but a leopard can't change its sports."

ॐ ॐ ॐ ॐ

What do you call a fish with no eyes?

A fsh

Bill and Ben were in the bath when Bill turns to Ben "Flobbalobbalob!" Ben looked at Bill in disgust and said, "If that smells, I'm gonna kill you!"

———————

What's the difference between a dead cat in the road and a dead lawyer in the road?

There are skid marks in front of the cat

How many Australian men does it take to change a light bulb?

100 – one to change the bulb and 99 to say, "Good on ya mate!"

What is the definition of a teenager?

God's punishment for enjoying sex too much

꾱꾱꾱꾱

Rob has a hot date with the office blonde bombshell Jenny and decides to go for a sunbed session to bronze his naked body. Unfortunately, he falls asleep under the sunbed and awakes to find his manhood reddened and stinging. nonetheless, he turns up for the date with Jenny and pretty soon they are back at Rob's flat, getting passionate on the couch, despite the fact that his willy was by this time burning like a bonfire.

"Excuse me a minute Jenny," said Rob, "I just need to go to the kitchen."

So Rob went in to the kitchen, poured himself a glass of milk, and deposited his throbbing manhood into the glass in an attempt to relieve the pain. Quite unexpectedly, Jenny appeared in the doorway looked at Rob and said, "So that's how you fill those things up!"

What's the difference between praying in church and praying at a race course?

At the race course you really mean it

A man walked into a doctor's surgery and says, "Doctor, I want a vasectomy as soon as possible."
"Hold on," said the doctor. "This is a big decision that you need to discuss with your family."
"I've already discussed it with my wife and children and we even had a democratic vote on it," said the man.
"And what was the result of that vote?" asked the doctor.
"Two against and twenty-seven for!" replied the man.

A woman is walking along a beach when she finds a lamp that she proceeds to rub vigorously. Out pops a genie who proclaims, "I will grant you three wishes, however there is a catch. Whatever wish I grant you, your ex-husband will get fivefold."
"Right, my first wish is for £10 million," said the woman.
"Your wish is granted," said the genie, "and now your ex-husband has £50 million."
"My second wish is to have a garage full of 20 top of the range sports cars," said the woman.
"Your wish is granted," said the genie, "and now your ex-husband has 100 sports cars. What is your last wish?"
After much deliberation the woman replies, "I'd like a mild heart attack."

A Red Indian chief lived to be 200 years-old and credited his longevity to his habit of drinking fifty cups of tea a day. Unfortunately he died on his 201st birthday after drowning in his own tea pee.

࿐ ࿐ ࿐ ࿐

How do porcupines make love?

Carefully

Why do footballers like intelligent women?

Because opposites attract

Female patient: Doctor, every time I sneeze I get multiple orgasms that engulf my entire body from tip to toe

Doctor: That's quite amazing, are you taking anything for it?

Patient: Yes extremely large doses of pepper

"Patient: Doctor, doctor today I feel like a tepee and yesterday I felt like a wigwam
Doctor: You're too tents"

Two men were drinking in the bar on the top floor of the Empire State Building, when one said to the other, "Do you know, the design of this building is a testament to the advances made by man in the world of architecture."

"Why's that?" asked the second man. "Because I can jump out of that window and halfway down the wind variations caused by the structure of the building will swirl me around the building and sweep me back inside."

"I don't believe it", said the second man. "Ok then, I'll show you," said his drinking partner and dived out of the window, circled the building three times before being swept back up and landing on his bar stool.

"I've got to give that a go!" said the second man. He dived out of the window and plummeted to the street below hitting the concrete with a sickening thud.

The barman shook his head ruefully and said, "Do you know Superman, you can be a proper arsehole when you've had a drink."

A little girl walked into her mother's bedroom and said, "Mummy, where do babies come from?" "Well darling, daddy puts his penis into my vagina and nine months later a baby appears," replied the mother. Her daughter looked puzzled before saying, "Last night I saw daddy put his penis in your mouth. Do babies come from there as well?" "No darling," replied the mother, "that's where jewellery comes from."

ॐ ॐ ॐ ॐ

Two guys drove right through a red light. "Man, you just ran that red light!" exclaimed the passenger. "Don't worry, my brother does it all the time," said the driver. They continued driving through town and then proceeded to drive through another red light.
"You just ran another red light! You're going to get us killed!" screamed the nervous passenger. "Don't worry, my brother does it all the time," repeated the driver. Moments later, they approached a green light and they came to a stop. "Why are you stopping?" asked the anxious passenger. The driver turned and said, "Because my brother might be coming!"

_____

What do you get if you cross a nettle with a four-leaf clover?

A rash of good luck

A man walks into a petrol station and buys a pack of cigarettes. He pulls one out and starts smoking it. The cashier says, "Excuse me Sir, but you can't smoke in here." The guy says, "Don't you think it's silly that I buy them here but can't smoke them here?" And the cashier replies, "Not really ... we also sell condoms."

ॐ ॐ ॐ ॐ

Two cows are standing next to each other in a field, Daisy says to Dolly, "I was artificially inseminated this morning."
"I don't believe you," says Dolly.
"It's true, straight up, no bull!"

"A man sees a friend in a bar, drinking by himself. Approaching the friend, he says, "You look terrible. What's the problem?"
"My mother died in June, and left me £10,000." said the friend. "Mate, I'm so sorry," he replied.
"Then in July," the friend continued, "My father died, leaving me £50,000." The man looking concerned says, "Two parents gone in two months. No wonder you're depressed." The friend continues, "And last month my aunt died, and left me £15,000." "Three close family members lost in three months? How sad!" "Then this month," continued the friend, "not a penny!"

In the forest, a little turtle began to climb a tree. After hours of effort, he reached the top, jumped into the air waving his front legs and crashed to the ground. After recovering, he slowly climbed the tree again, jumped, and fell to the ground. The turtle tried again and again, while a couple of birds sitting on a branch watched his sad efforts. Finally, the female bird turned to her mate. "Dear," she chirped, "I think it's time to tell him he's adopted."

ॐ ॐ ॐ ॐ

What's a man's definition of a romantic evening?

Sex

> A man walks into a dentist's and asks how much it costs to extract wisdom teeth. "£80," the dentist says. "Isn't there a cheaper way?" asks the man. "Well," the dentist says, "if you don't use an anaesthetic, I can knock it down to £60." The man says, "That's still too expensive!" "OK," says the dentist. "If I just rip the teeth out with a pair of pliers, I can knock it down to £20." "Nope, it's still too much." "Well," says the dentist, "if I let one of my students do it, I suppose I can knock the price down to £10." "Marvellous," says the man, "book my wife in for next Tuesday!"

A traffic policeman noticed a car driving erratically and set off in pursuit. He flagged the driver down and pulled his car in front. He approached the car and said to the driver, "Do you mind stepping out of the car please, Sir?" The policeman then asked the driver, "Could you blow into this bag please Sir." "I can't do that," replied the driver.

"And why not?" asked the policeman. The driver replied, "Because I suffer from asthma." The policeman then said, "In that case, you'll have to provide a urine sample at the station." "I can't do that. I'm diabetic and I suffer from low blood sugar."

"In that case," said the policeman, "you'll have to provide a blood sample." "I can't do that," replied the driver. "And why not" asked the policeman. The driver replied, "Because I'm a haemophiliac."

"In that case," said the policeman, "I will have to ask you to walk along this straight line down the centre of the road without stepping off it." "I can't do that," replied the driver. "And why not?" asked the policeman.

The driver replied, "Because I'm pissed."

A husband and wife were chatting in bed when the husband asked, "What is it that you like about me, is it my trim muscular frame?"

"No," replied the wife.

"Then is it my unparalleled sexual technique?" he asked.

"No," replied the wife.

"Is it my loving and patient nature?" asked the husband.

"No," replied the wife.

"Then it must be my superior intellect," said her husband.

"No," replied his wife, "it's your sense of humour."

ॐ ॐ ॐ ॐ

Why do blondes have more fun?

They are much easier to keep amused

A psychiatrist is holding a seminar for mothers and their children and after examining his notes began the proceedings by announcing, "All the people present here today suffer from obsessions which they have passed on to their children." He went on to say, "Mrs Brown, you have an obsession with gambling and you have even named your daughter Penny. Mrs Smith, you have an obsession with drinking and have even named your daughter Sherry. Mrs Cooper, you have an obsession with eating and have even named your daughter Candy."

At which point Mrs Williams gets to her feet, grabs her son by the hand and says, "Enough of this Dick, we're going home."

_____

A 50-year-old tail-less elephant was walking through the jungle with his friend, the tiger, when a turtle crossed their paths. The elephant picked up the turtle with his trunk, swung it around his head several times and threw it against a nearby tree, laughing as its shell smashed into thousands of tiny pieces. The tiger was visibly shocked at this out of character display and asked the elephant, "Why did you do that?" The elephant replied, "When I was a six month-old calf, that very same turtle bit off my tail." The tiger was suitably impressed and said, "It really is true that elephants never forget. You really do possess the most wonderful memory." "Turtle recall!" replied the elephant.

Wendy and Joe had been married for 50 years. One day Wendy was cleaning the attic and found an egg box containing three eggs and £1000. She went to ask Joe for an explanation. "I cannot tell a lie," said Joe. "Every time I have been unfaithful I placed an egg in this box."
"Well I am very hurt," said Mary, "but I don't suppose three affairs in a 50-year marriage is too bad, but where did the £1000 come from?"
"It's like this Mary, every time I got a dozen eggs I sold them."

What is the definition of a
beauty parlour?

A place where women curl up
and dye

ॐॐॐॐ

**Harry's wife says, "Harry, do
these jeans make my ass look
like the side of the house?"
He looks down and says,
"Of course not darling, our
house isn't blue."**

———————

Bill and Madge were sitting at their breakfast table
celebrating their fiftieth wedding anniversary. Madge
looked into Bill's eyes and said, "Do you know Bill, 50 years
ago we would have sat here completely naked."

Bill replied, "There's nothing to stop us reliving our
youth," and both began shedding their clothes. As they
sat there naked, Madge whispered to Bill seductively,
"Do you know Bill, my nipples are as hot for you now as
they were 50 years ago."

"I'm not surprised," said Bill, "one of them is in the teapot
and the other's in your porridge."

"Doctor, doctor, I think I'm a mouth organ."

"That's strange, a female patient said the same thing to me yesterday."

"Yes, that would be our Monica!"

After she woke up, a woman told her husband, "I just dreamt that you gave me a diamond necklace for Valentine's day. What do you think it means?"

"You'll know tonight," he said. That evening, the man came home with a small package and gave it to his wife. Delighted, she opened it – to find a book entitled *The Meaning of Dreams*.

ॐॐॐॐ

How is Colonel Sanders like a typical man?

All he's concerned with is legs, breasts and thighs

> A blind man was travelling in his private jet when he detected something was wrong. He made his way to the cockpit and got no response from his pilot.
>
> The blind guy then found the radio and started calling the tower for help. The tower came back and asked, "What's the problem?"
>
> The blind guy yelled, "Help me! I'm blind, the pilot is dead, and we're flying upside down!"
>
> The tower came back and asked, "How do you know you're upside down?" "Because the shit is running down my back!"

A man came round in hospital after a serious accident. He shouted, "Doctor, doctor, I can't feel my legs!" The doctor replied, "I know you can't, I had to cut your arms off."

Two Eskimos were sat in their igloo when one turned to the other and asked, "What's the best way of catching a polar bear?" His friend replied, "What you should do is cut a big hole in the ice and wait for a polar bear to come along. When he sees the hole he will bend over to look into it for fish. Then you quickly run up behind him and kick him in the ice hole."

Sherlock Holmes and Dr Watson were out camping. They had retired for the night when Watson was woken up with a nudge. "Tell me, Watson," said Holmes, "what do you see?" Watson looked skywards and said, "I see that Mars is in juxtaposition with Venus, that leads me to deduce that a meteorite storm may fall to Earth. I see a full Moon and it has been proven that criminal activity increases during this cycle. Therefore I deduce that when we return to Baker Street our workload will increase. I see a starry night and therefore I deduce that there will be a morning frost. What do you see Holmes?" Holmes replied, "Elementary my dear Watson, I deduce that some bugger has stolen our tent!"

Bill had not had a good day when he answered a knock at the door. He opened the door to a snail who pleaded, "Can I come in please?" Bill's temper got the better of him and he gave the snail a hefty kick and watched it sail down the garden path and over the garden gate. A week later there was another knock at the door and Bill answered the door to be greeted by the snail.

The irate mollusc glared at Bill and said, "What did you do that for?"

Two aerials met on a roof, fell in love and got married.

The ceremony was rubbish but the reception was brilliant.

On the first day of college, the dean addressed the students, pointing out some of the rules: "The female halls will be out-of-bounds for all male students, and the male halls to the female students. Anybody caught breaking this rule will be fined £20. Anybody caught breaking this rule a second time will be fined £60. Being caught a third time will cost you £180. Are there any questions?" "How much for a season ticket?"

A man was sunbathing on holiday when a lifeguard with a huge bulge down his trunks walked by. The lifeguard was quickly surrounded by women and he led his new-found admirers to a nearby beachside bar. The sunbather followed and sat next to the lifeguard and whispered, "How do you manage to attract all these women?"

The lifeguard looked at him and said, "I'll let you into a secret. I have a cucumber shoved down my trunks."

The man listened intently, then rose from his seat and walked to the supermarket where he purchased a cucumber. He returned to the beach with the cucumber down his trunks and strutted past a group of sunbathing women giving them a wink. The women jumped to their feet and ran screaming in the opposite direction. Perplexed, he walked away dejected, when he felt a tap on his shoulder. He turned to be faced with the lifeguard who said to him, "You're supposed to put the cucumber down the front of your trunks!"

Three men, Tom, Dick and Harry were sat in a pub sipping their beers and discussing the utter stupidity of their respective wives.

Tom said, "My wife is the most stupid woman in the world. Last week she spent £100 on meat because of a special offer at the supermarket, despite the fact that we are vegetarians!"

Dick retorted, "That's nothing, my wife spent £15,000 on a car and neither of us can drive!"

Harry spoke up, "I can beat the pair of you," he said. "Last week my wife spent £1000 on a holiday to Benidorm. Yesterday I saw her packing her case and noticed ten packets of condoms in the side pocket and she doesn't even have a penis!"

ॐ ॐ ॐ ॐ

Little Billy was in his back garden filling in a large hole he had just dug. His neighbour peered over the back garden fence and said, "Good morning Billy, what are you doing?"

Billy replied, "My pet gerbil Jimmy has died and I'm burying him."

"That's rather a large hole for a gerbil isn't it?" enquired the neighbour.

"Yes," said Billy, "that's because he's inside your bloody cat!"

———————

What did Snow White say to Pinocchio when she sat on his face?

"Lie, you bastard, lie!"

John returned home early from work one day to find his wife lying naked on the bed and gasping for air. "What's wrong with you?" he asked in a concerned tone. "I think I'm having a heart attack," she gasped. John hurtled down the stairs to phone for an ambulance when his son Teddy tugged on his arm and said, "Daddy, Uncle Frank is upstairs in your wardrobe with no clothes on." John rushed upstairs, yanked open the wardrobe door and yelled, "For Christ's sake, Frank, the wife's having a heart attack and you're running around naked scaring the kids."

ॐॐॐॐ

Two women were talking about the new hunk in the neighbourhood. "But he's so stupid," said one to the other. "I think he must have his brains between his legs." "Yeah," her friend sighed, "but I'd sure love to blow his mind."

———————

Two hillbillies are walking towards each other, and one is carrying a sack. When they meet, one says, "Hey, Tommy Ray, what'cha got in the bag?" "Jes' some chickens." "If I guesses how many they is, kin I have one?" "Shoot, if ya guesses right, I'll give you both of 'em!" "OK. Ummmmm ... five?"

Ken was at work when his best friend Richard called round at his house. Ken's wife Barbara answered the door and invited Richard in. Barbara was quite taken aback when Richard blurted out, "I have always fancied you, there is nothing I would like more than to carry you to the bedroom and make love to you right now!"

"I can't do that, you're Ken's best friend!" said Barbara. "What if I gave you £500? Would that persuade you?" asked Richard.

"It would," said Barbara unashamedly, and she took the money before they both disappeared to the bedroom.

Four hours later Ken arrived home from work. "Barbara darling, has Richard called round?" he asked.

"Yes," said Barbara sheepishly fearing the worst.

"Good man," said Ken, "and did he give you the £500 that he owes me?"

Did you hear about the dyslexic devil worshipper who sold his soul to Santa?

࿓࿓࿓࿓

What has five fingers and drives a tractor?

A farmhand

Scientist have discovered that beer contains minute traces of the female gene. In order to prove their discovery they gave a group of men 20 pints of beer each to drink. The theory was proved when after the experiment 100% of the drinkers began talking rubbish and were incapable of driving.

࿓࿓࿓࿓

A man walked into a psychiatrist's office completely naked, with the exception of a roll of cellophane wrapped around his groin area.
The psychiatrist looked up from the papers he was reading and gazed at the man with a knowing smile before saying, "I can clearly see your nuts."

A termite walks into a bar and asks, "Is the bar tender here?"

_____

A man walks into a pub and orders a pint of lager and a packet of helicopter flavoured crisps. The barman replies, "Sorry sir we've only got plane."

A beautiful blonde walked into a doctor's surgery. The doctor gazed at the lady as she sat in the chair opposite and gave him a seductive smile. He gawped at her long legs, full firm breasts and ruby red lips. "How can I help you?" asked the doctor.

"I have a problem with my breasts," replied the blonde. "Remove your clothes then," said the doctor, "so I can examine you." The woman slowly unbuttoned her blouse and unhooked her bra to reveal the most exquisite breasts the doctor had ever set eyes on.

"And what seems to be the problem?" asked the doctor. The patient replied, "Whenever I talk to a stranger my nipples go hard."

"I'm not sure what the problem is," said the doctor, "but I think it's contagious."

Ways For A Man To Impress A Woman

Shower her with loving
care and attention
Wine and dine her and buy
her expensive gifts even
when it's not her birthday
Bring her breakfast in bed on
a tray with a vase containing
a single red rose
Every day tell her how much
you love her and how much
she means to you
Let her watch home improvement
TV shows even when football is
on the other side

Ways For A Woman To Impress A Man

Turn up naked
Bring beer

ॐ ॐ ॐ ॐ

How do you make a snooker table laugh?

**Put your hand in its pocket
and tickle its balls**

_____

In the first year of marriage, the
man speaks and the woman
listens. In the second year,
the woman speaks and the
man listens. In the third year,
they both speak and the
neighbours listen.

What do you call a man with a toilet on his head?

Lou

ॐ ॐ ॐ ॐ

How can you tell when a man is well hung?

When you can just barely slip your finger in between his neck and the noose

A drunk walked into a pub and said to the landlord, "Excuse me do you mind if I use your toilet?"

"Not at all," said the landlord, "it's the second door on the right."

The drunk staggered away and in his drunken state, walked through the second door on the left where he was greeted with a magnificent-looking golden toilet. He sat on the toilet and let nature take its course. The following day the drunk staggered back into the pub and asked the landlord, "Excuse me, do you mind if I use your golden toilet again?" The landlord smiled before shouting, "Hey Bob, I think we've found the idiot who crapped in your tuba."

A grandfather was babysitting his grandson when he noticed him pulling a worm from the flowerbed. "I bet you £5 you can't put that back in the hole it came from" said the grandfather.
"You're on," said his grandson and he ran into the house, returning with a can of aerosol. He proceeded to spray the worm, which immediately stiffened, allowing him to replace it in the hole. His disgruntled grandfather paid him the £5 and walked back into the house with the aerosol. One hour later the grandfather came back outside and gave his grandson another £5. "But grandad, you've already paid me" said the boy. "That £5 is off your grandmother."

Husband: Shall we try a different position tonight?

Wife: That's a good idea ... you stand by the ironing board while I sit on the sofa and fart

———————————

The new employee stood before the paper shredder looking confused. "Need some help?" asked a secretary, walking by. "Yes," he replied, "how does this thing work?" "Simple," she said, taking the fat report from his hand and feeding it into the shredder. "Thanks, but where do the copies come out?"

ॐ ॐ ॐ ॐ

A man lay sprawled across three seats in the theatre. When the usher came by, he told the man, "Sorry sir, but you're only allowed one seat." The man groaned but didn't budge. The usher became impatient. "Sir, if you don't get up from there I'm going to have to call the manager." Again, the man groaned, which infuriated the usher who marched back up the aisle. In a few moments, the usher and the manager returned and stood over the man. Together the two of them tried and failed to move him. Finally, they summoned the police. The policeman surveyed the situation then asked, "OK pal, what's your name?" "Sam," the man moaned. "Where are you from, Sam?" With pain in his voice Sam replied "The balcony."

A husband woke up one night with a huge erection and nudged his wife hopefully. His wife woke up and said, "What is it?" "I'm feeling randy," said the husband, "can we make love?" "No darling, you know I have an appointment with the gynaecologist tomorrow and I want to stay nice and fresh" said the wife.
The husband turned his back on her and five minutes later nudged her again and asked, "Darling, you wouldn't happen to have an appointment with the dentist as well would you?"

A doctor was walking down a hospital corridor when a nurse approached him and said, "Doctor, could you please sign this medical report?" The doctor reached in his pocket, pulled out a thermometer and exclaimed, "Oh no, some arsehole's got my pen!"

If mothers have Mother's Day and fathers have Father's Day, what do single men have?

Palm Sunday

ॐ ॐ ॐ ॐ

What is an ig?

An Eskimo's home minus a toilet!

What's the difference between a woman and a computer?

A computer doesn't laugh at 3½ inch floppies

_____

ॐ ॐ ॐ ॐ

How can you tell if a moth has farted?

It flies in a straight line

Two cannibals are eating a clown, when one says to the other, "Can you taste something funny?"

What's the only thing worse than a male chauvinist pig?

A woman who won't do as she's told

༃ ༃ ༃ ༃

Why do women have small feet?

So they can stand closer to the sink

How many paranoid electricians does it take to change a light bulb?

Who wants to know?

What's the difference between a boyfriend and a husband?

About 60 minutes

———————

 What's the best way of annoying your wife during sex?

Phone her

> Through the pitch-black night, the captain sees a light straight ahead on a collision course with his ship. He sends a signal: Change your course ten degree east.
>
> The light signals back: Change your course, ten degrees west.
>
> Angry, the captain sends: I'm a navy captain! Change your course, Sir!
>
> I'm a seaman, second class, comes the reply. Change your course, Sir.
>
> Now the captain is furious. I'm a battleship! I'm not changing course!
>
> There is one last reply. I'm a lighthouse. It's your call.

Walking up to a department store's fabric counter, a pretty girl said, "I would like to buy this material for a new dress. How much does it cost?" "Only one kiss per yard," replied the male clerk with a smirk. "That's fine," said the girl, "I'll take ten yards." With expectation and anticipation written all over his face, the clerk quickly measured out the cloth, wrapped it up, then teasingly held it out. The girl snapped up the package, pointed to the old geezer standing beside her, and smiled, "My grandad is paying."

৯৯৯৯

What's the difference between a saxophone player and a lawn mower?

One cuts grass and the other smokes it

ॐ ॐ ॐ ॐ

What is black and white and cries?

A pregnant nun

In a recent university experiment, four worms were placed in four separate bottles.

The first bottle was full of beer, the second bottle was full of cigar smoke, the third bottle was full of sperm and the last bottle was full of soil.

After one week the worms in the beer bottle, the cigar smoke bottle and the sperm bottle were all dead.

However, the worm in the bottle full of soil was alive and kicking.

CONCLUSION: If you drink, smoke and have sex you won't get worms!

Terry goes for his first day working at a big "everything under one roof" store. After the store was locked up at night, the boss came down. "How many sales did you make today?" Terry says, "One." The boss was furious, "Just one? Our sales people average 20 or 30 sales a day. How much was the sale for?" Terry replied "£101,237.64." The boss says, "£101,237.64? What the hell did you sell?"

Terry told him, "First, I sold him a small fish hook. Then, I sold him a medium fish hook. Then, I sold him a large fish hook. Then, I sold him a new fishing rod. Then, I asked him where he was going fishing and he said down to the coast, so I told him he was gonna need a boat, so we went down to the boat department and I sold him that twin engine. Then he said he didn't think his car would pull it, so I took him down to the automotive department and I sold him that 4X4."

The boss said, "A guy came in here to buy a fish hook and you sold him a boat and a truck?" Terry says, "No, he came in here to buy a box of tampons for his wife and I said, 'Well, your weekend's buggered, you might as well go fishing.'"

A paper bag walked into the doctor's and was greeted by the grim-faced medic.
"I'm afraid I have some bad news for you" said the doctor. "You appear to have contracted AIDS."
"That's impossible," cried the paper bag, "I've never had any form of sexual contact, nor am I a drug user!"
"In that case," said the doctor, "your father must be a carrier."

ক্ষতক্ষতক্ষতক্ষত

What do you call a woman with a sinking ship on her head?

Mandy Lifeboats

Reaching the end of a job interview, the Human Resources person asked a young engineer, "And what starting salary were you looking for?" The engineer said, "In the region of £125,000 a year, depending on the benefits package."
The interviewer said, "Well, what would you say to a package of five weeks holiday, fourteen paid holidays, full medical and dental, a company matching retirement fund for 50% of your salary, and a company car leased every 2 years – say, a Porsche?"
The engineer sat up straight and said, "Wow! Are you kidding?"
And the interviewer replied, "Yeah, but you started it!"

ক্ষতক্ষতক্ষতক্ষত

A man comes home from an exhausting day at work, sits down in front of the television, and tells his wife, "Get me a beer before it starts." The wife sighs and gets him a beer. Soon after, he says, "Get me another beer before it starts." She looks cross, but fetches another beer and slams it down next to him. He finishes that beer and a few minutes later says, "Quick, get me another beer, it's going to start any minute." The wife is furious. She yells at him "Is that all you're going to do tonight? Drink beer and sit in front of that TV? You're nothing but a lazy, drunken, fat slob, and furthermore ..."
The man sighs and says, "It's started ..."

_____

How is playing bagpipes like throwing a javelin blindfolded?

You don't have to be very good to get people's attention

ॐॐॐॐ

What do you call a man with a car on his head?

Jack

Several men are in the changing room of a golf club. A mobile phone on a bench rings and a man engages the hands-free speaker function and begins to talk. Everyone else in the room stops to listen.

MAN: "Hello?"

WOMAN: "Hi honey. I'm at the shopping centre and found this beautiful coat. It's only £1000. Is it OK if I buy it?"

MAN: "Sure, go ahead if you like it that much."

WOMAN: "I also stopped by the Mercedes dealership and saw the new models. I saw one I really liked."

MAN: "How much?"

WOMAN: "£60,000."

MAN: "OK, but for that price I want it with all the options."

WOMAN: "Fantastic! Oh, and one more thing ... the house we wanted last year is back on the market. They're asking £950,000."

MAN: "Well, then go ahead and give them an offer, but just offer £900,000."

WOMAN: "OK. I'll see you later! I love you!"

MAN: "Bye, I love you, too."

The man hangs up. The other men in the locker room are looking at him in astonishment. Then he asks: "Anyone know whose phone this is?"

What do you call a blonde with two brain cells?

Pregnant

Three pregnant women, a blonde, a brunette and a redhead were sitting in a doctor's waiting room. The brunette said, "I'm going to have a girl, because when the baby was conceived I was on top." The redhead said, "I'm going to have a boy, because when the baby was conceived I was on the bottom." "Oh my God!" shrieked the blonde. "Does that mean I'm going to have a puppy?"

ॐ ॐ ॐ ॐ

A man walked into a pub with a dead swan and ordered a beer. He sat down at a table, sipped his drink and pulled off one of the swan's wings and began to eat it. Five minutes later he took another sip of his beer and began to eat one of the swan's legs. Ten minutes later he began munching on the swan's neck. The barman noticed he had almost finished his drink and asked, "Would you like another one?" "No thanks" said the man, "I'm just having this swan then I'm going."

A timid little man ventured into a biker bar in the Bronx and clearing his throat asked, "Um, er, which of you gentlemen owns the Doberman tied outside?"
A giant of a man, wearing leathers, his body hair growing out through the seams, turned slowly, looked down at the quivering little man and said, "It's my dog. Why?"
"Well," squeaked the little man, "I believe my dog just killed it."
"What?" roared the big man. "What in the hell kind of dog do you have?"
"It's a little four-week-old poodle puppy" answered the little man, "Bull!" roared the biker, "How could your puppy kill my Doberman?"
"It appears that your dog choked on her, Sir."

Why do only 10% of men make it to heaven?

Because if they all went, it would be hell

Justin the cannibal was in his kitchen preparing a leg of human when there was a knock at the door. He opened the door to find his friend Tom standing there, "Good morning Tom" said Justin. "What's the matter?"
"I've just dumped my girlfriend," said Tom. "How can I help?"
To which Tom replied, "I was wondering if I could borrow some toilet paper?"

When Albert Einstein was making the rounds of the speaker's circuit, he usually found himself longing to get back to his lab work. One night as they were driving to yet another dinner, Einstein mentioned to his chauffeur (a man who somewhat resembled Einstein in looks and manner) that he was tired of speechmaking.

"I have an idea, boss," his chauffeur said. "I've heard you give this speech so many times. I'll bet I could give it for you." Einstein laughed loudly and said, "Why not? Let's do it!" When they arrived at the dinner, Einstein donned the chauffeur's cap and jacket and sat at the back of the room. The chauffeur gave a beautiful rendition of the speech and even answered a few questions expertly.

Then a pompous professor asked an extremely esoteric question about anti-matter formation, digressing here and there to let everyone in the audience know that he was nobody's fool. Without missing a beat, the chauffeur fixed the professor with a steely stare and said, "Sir, the answer to that question is so simple that I will let my chauffeur, who is sitting in the back, answer it for me."

A barman is working, when this really sexy lady walks up and says in a seductive voice, "May I please speak to your manager?" He says, "Not right now, is there anything I can help you with?" She replies, "I don't know if you're the man to talk to ... it's kind of personal ..." Thinking he might get lucky, he says, "I'm pretty sure I can handle your problem, Miss." She then looks at him with a smile, and puts two of her fingers in his mouth ... and he begins sucking them, thinking, "I'm in!" She says, "Can you give the manager something for me?" The barman nods ... yes. "Tell him there's no toilet paper in the ladies' toilets."

ॐ ॐ ॐ ॐ

Why don't blondes eat bananas?

They can't find the zip

What do you call a man with a spade on his head?

Doug

What do you call a man without a spade on his head?

Douglas

A woman was strolling across a golf course when she noticed a group of men standing in a circle. She approached the scene and saw they were surrounding a young man who was in agony with his hands clasped between his thighs. "What happened to you?" she enquired. Between his moans the man gasped, "I've been struck by a stray ball." "Let me have a look," said the woman. She pulled down his zip and placed her hand inside the hole and proceeded to massage the area. "How does that feel?" she asked. "That feels just great," said the man, "but my thumb still hurts like hell."

A man was sitting in the waiting room of a doctor's surgery whilst his wife was being treated.
He was most disturbed when his wife burst out of the surgery crying. "What's wrong darling?" he asked her.
The wife replied, "The doctor was examining me and he told me I had a pretty fanny."
Her husband stormed into the doctor's surgery and yelled, "What the hell do you think you're playing at, telling my wife she has a pretty fanny?"
"Calm down," said the doctor, "your wife misunderstood me. What I actually said was that she has acute angina."

———————

Jones came into the office an hour late and found the boss waiting for him. "What's the story this time, Jones?" he asked. "Let's hear a good excuse for a change." Jones sighed, "Everything went wrong this morning, boss. The wife decided to drive me to the station. She got ready in ten minutes, but then there was an accident on the bridge. Rather than let you down, I swam across the river – look, my suit's still damp – ran out to the airport, got a ride on Mr Thompson's helicopter, landed on top of the town hall, and was carried here piggyback by one of The Spice Girls." "You'll have to do better than that, Jones" said the boss, obviously disappointed. "No woman can get ready in ten minutes."

A man limps into a bar with a cane and alligator. The barman says "Hold on, you can't bring that in here, they aren't allowed!" So the man says, "But my 'gator does a really cool trick ..." The barman says, "Well then, let's see." So the man whips out his dick and shoves it in the 'gator's mouth. He then takes his cane and starts bashing the 'gator on the head. A crowd grows and everyone is astonished when he pulls out his dick without a single scratch.

He looks around the crowd and says, "Does anyone else want to try?" An old lady raises her hand and says "Sure, but don't hit me with that stick."

A jockey is about to enter an important race on a new horse. The horse's trainer meets him before the race and says, "Just remember with this horse, when you approach a jump, you have to shout, 'ALLLLEEE OOOP!' loudly in the horse's ear. If you do that, you'll be fine."

The race begins and they approach the first hurdle. The jockey ignores the trainer's advice and the horse crashes straight through the fence. They carry on and approach the second. The jockey, embarrassed, whispers 'Aleeee ooop' in the horse's ear. The same thing happens – the horse crashes straight through the centre of the fence.

At the third hurdle, the jockey thinks, "It's no good, I'll have to do it," and yells, "ALLLEEE OOOP!" really loudly. Sure enough, the horse sails over the jump with no problems. This continues for the rest of the race, but due to the poor start the horse only finishes third.

The trainer is fuming and asks the jockey what went wrong. The jockey replies, "Nothing's wrong with me – it's this bloody horse. What is he – deaf or something?"

The trainer replies, "Deaf? DEAF? He's not deaf – he's BLIND!"

Three young boys are sitting in a tree house boasting about their father's smoking prowess. The first boy says, "My father smokes cigarettes and he can blow smoke rings and loads of other shapes out of his mouth." The second boy says, "That's nothing, my dad smokes a pipe and can blow smoke out of his ears." The third boy says, "I can beat that, my father smokes cigars and he can blow smoke out of his bum." "Really," said the other boys, "have you seen him do it?" "No," came the reply, "but I've seen the tobacco stains on his boxer shorts."

ॐ ॐ ॐ ॐ

Why is a drum machine better than a drummer?

It can keep a steady beat and it won't sleep with your girlfriend

——————

What do you call a man with a rabbit on his head?

Warren

Rosie had passed away and John called 999. The operator told John that she would send someone out right away. "Where do you live?" asked the operator. John replied, "At the end of Eucalyptus Drive." The operator asked, "Can you spell that for me?" After a long pause, John said, "How about I drag her over to Oak Street and you pick her up there?"

ॐ ॐ ॐ ॐ

What's the difference between God and a lawyer?

God doesn't think he's a lawyer

_____

"

A man with a brain tumour visited a surgeon who had developed a revolutionary operation involving transplants. On meeting the surgeon the man asked how much the brains costed. The surgeon replied, "For a man, I must transplant a man's brain into your skull and that will be £1000." "Fine" said the man. "Just out of interest, how much are women's brains?" "Women's brains are £100," said the surgeon. "So tell me," the man asked curiously, "why are women's brains a tenth of the price of men's brains?" The surgeon replied, "Because they've been used."

"

Two bags of vomit were sliding down the street, when one of them suddenly burst into tears. The other bag of vomit looked at him confused and said, "What's the matter with you?" The bag wiped away his tears and snuffled, "This is where I was brought up."

৯৯৯৯

What do you call a sheep with no legs?

A cloud

A little girl was talking to her teacher about whales.

The teacher said it was impossible for a whale to swallow a human because even though a whale is a very large mammal, its throat is very small.
The little girl stated that Jonah was swallowed by a whale.

The teacher reiterated that a whale could not swallow a human, it was impossible.

The girl said, "When I get to heaven I will ask Jonah."

The teacher asked, "What if Jonah went to hell?"

The little girl replied, "Then you ask him!"

A woman went to a fancy dress party completely naked save for a pair of black gloves and a pair of black socks. The host asked her, "What on earth have you come as?" She replied "The five of spades."

A young blonde was walking down the street with her right breast hanging out of her blouse. A policeman saw the young lady and strolled over to her before saying, "Excuse me Miss, but do you realise that your breast is showing and I could arrest you for indecent exposure?" "Oh my god!" screamed the blonde. "I've left my baby on the bus again!"

Superman was flying over Metropolis dodging the skyscrapers. He swooped upwards and surveyed the city with his x-ray vision. Four blocks away on the rooftop of a skyscraper he spied Wonder Woman who was sunbathing in the nude. The man of steel thought to himself, I can fly down there at super speed and bonk my old friend Wonder Woman. I'll be able to fly away before she realises what has happened. So Superman hurtled towards his prey, with his pants around his ankles, entered the super heroine and after numerous thrusts in super quick time flew off again. "What the hell was that?" cried Wonder Woman. "I don't know" said the Invisible Man, "but my arse hurts like hell."

ॐ ॐ ॐ ॐ

What's grey and comes in bucketfuls?

An elephant

_____

What's a leper's favourite sport?

Football

☙☙☙☙

It was the first day back at school after Christmas and Miss Jones, the class teacher, asked little Tommy what Santa Claus brought him.

"I got a bow wow," said Tommy.

"No Tommy, you got a dog," scolded the teacher. "You are old enough now to start using grown-up language. What else did you get?"

"I got a choo choo," replied Tommy.

"No, you did not," said Miss Jones becoming increasingly irritated, "you got a train. What else did you get?"

"I got a book," said Tommy.

"What was the title of the book?" asked the teacher.

After much deliberation Tommy replied, "Winnie the shit."

A young man, who was an avid golfer, found himself with a few hours to spare one afternoon. He figured if he hurried and played fast, he could get in nine holes before heading home. As he was about to tee off, an old man shuffled onto the tee and asked if he could accompany the young man, as he was golfing alone. Not being able to say no, he allowed the old man to join him. To his surprise, the old man played fairly quickly. He didn't hit the ball far, but plodded along consistently and didn't waste much time. Finally, they reached the ninth fairway and the young man found himself with a tough shot. There was a large pine tree right in front of his ball and directly between his ball and the green. After several minutes of debating how to hit the shot, the old man finally said, "You know, when I was your age, I'd hit the ball right over that tree."

With that challenge placed before him, the youngster swung hard, hit the ball up, right smack into the top of the tree trunk and it thudded back on the ground by his feet. The old man offered one more comment, "Of course, when I was your age, that pine tree was only 3 feet tall."

The seven dwarfs were attending mass at church and when it was over Dopey sidled up to Father Jones and said, "Excuse me Father, I hope you don't mind me asking, but are there any 4-foot nuns working in this church?" Father Jones replied, "No Dopey, we have no nuns of that height working here." "Then tell me," said Dopey, "are there any 4-foot nuns at all who live or work in this town?" "None at all Dopey," said the father. The other six dwarfs burst into laughter before breaking into a chorus of, "Dopey shagged a penguin, Dopey shagged a penguin."

ॐ ॐ ॐ ॐ

What do your boss and a slinky have in common?

They're both fun to watch tumble down the stairs

A lady lost her handbag during a day of shopping. It was found by an honest little boy and returned to her. Looking in her purse, she commented, "Hmmm ... That's funny. When I lost my bag there was a £20 note in it. Now there are 20 pound coins." The boy quickly replied, "That's right. The last time I found a lady's purse, she didn't have change for a reward."

What do you call 100 lawyers at the bottom of the ocean?

A good start

———————

A woman stood in front of the mirror, complaining to her husband that her breasts were too small. The husband came up with a suggestion: "If you want your breasts to grow, try rubbing toilet paper between them for a few seconds." The wife asked "How will that make them bigger?" Without missing a beat the husband said, "I don't know, but it worked for your arse."

ॐ ॐ ॐ ॐ

"

Larry's barn burned down and his wife, Susan, called the insurance company.

Susan told the insurance company, "We had that barn insured for £50,000 and I want my money."

The agent replied, "Whoa there, just a minute, Susan. Insurance doesn't work quite like that. We will ascertain the value of what was insured and provide you with a new one of comparable worth."

There was a long pause before Susan replied, "Then I'd like to cancel the policy on my husband."

"

One day a man decided to buy a farm. He found the perfect place and put in an offer. The farmer said "Yeah, I'll sell it to you, but first there are four things you need to know: a rooster is called a cock: a wagon is called a pullet: a donkey is called an ass: and when the donkey starts acting up all you have to do is smack it." Within a couple of days the man had the farm. He was walking down the road with the rooster, donkey and wagon, when suddenly the donkey started acting up. He looked up and saw a woman approaching him. He stopped the woman and said, "Excuse me miss, will you hold my cock and pullet while I smack my ass?"

ॐ ॐ ॐ ॐ

"

A man picked up a woman at a disco and took her back to his flat. In no time at all they were having sex. After the deed was completed the woman said to the man, "You're a dentist aren't you?"

"As it happens I am," replied the man. "How did you know that?"

"Because all night long you've been washing your hands," she replied. "And what's more you're a very good dentist aren't you?"

"As it happens I am," he replied. "How did you know that?"

To which she replied, "Because I didn't feel a thing!"

"

A jelly baby walked into a doctor's surgery and upon examining the sweet the doctor proclaimed, "It appears that you have contracted a number of sexually transmitted diseases." "I'm not surprised," replied the jelly baby, "I've been going to bed with all sorts"

Always borrow money from a pessimist – they don't expect it back!

ॐॐॐॐ

What do you call a man who's lost 99% of his intelligence?

Divorced

How do you find a blind man on a nudist beach?

It's not very hard!

_____

An old man walked into a chemist's and enquired of the young assistant, "Do you sell Viagra?" "Yes Sir," replied the assistant, "and it will help with any erection problems." "Will I be able to get it over the counter?" asked the old man. "Probably," replied the assistant, "if you take three tablets all at once."

ॐॐॐॐ

What has 90 balls and screws
old ladies?

A bingo machine

ॐॐॐॐ

**What do you call a fly with
no wings?**

A walk

Why do men prefer
showers to baths?

Because peeing in the bath
is a disgusting habit

Why do moths fly with their
legs open?

Have you seen the size of
mothballs?

ॐॐॐॐ

" What would you do with
365 used condoms?

Melt them down, make
a tyre and call it
a good year **"**

What do you call a man with a Sherman tank on his head?

Dead

Two men were in a pub discussing unusual sexual positions. The first man said, "The most unusual sexual position I know is the rodeo position." "How does that work?" asked his drinking buddy. "It's a bit like doggy style," he replied. "The only difference is, halfway through the act you lean forward and whisper into your partner's ear, 'this is your mother's favourite position too.' Then you brace yourself and try to hang on for ten seconds."

Two blondes jumped off of a cliff. One of them had two budgerigars fastened to each arm, whilst the other had two parrots fastened to each arm. As they plunged towards the ground the first blonde said to the second, "I don't think much of this budgie jumping." "I agree," replied her friend. "And this parrot gliding ain't much fun either."

A woman woke up one morning and opened her bedroom curtains. She was shocked to find a gorilla sitting in a tree in her garden. She immediately ran downstairs and searched out her Yellow Pages.

After flicking through the book she came upon an advert reading, Tex Dermist: Unwanted Animals Removed. She rang the number and explained her predicament and 30 minutes later a grizzly-looking man arrived carrying a shotgun and holding a Doberman on a lead.

The lady showed the man the ape in her tree and said to him, "Will you be able to get it down?"

"Here's how it works," said Tex. "You take the shotgun and I climb up the tree and shake the branches. The gorilla will fall out of the tree and my Doberman has been specially trained to bite the bollocks off its prey."

"That sounds a little extreme," said the shocked woman, "but what's the shotgun for?"

Tex replied, "If I fall out of the tree first, shoot the dog!"

Produced by Miles Kelly Publishing Ltd, Bardfield Centre,
Great Bardfield, Essex, England CM7 4SL

Produced for Advanced Marketing (UK) Ltd, Bicester, Oxon

2 4 6 8 10 9 7 5 3 1

Editorial Director
Anne Marshall

Project Management
Mark Darling

Cover Design
Debbie Meekcoms

Production
Estela Godoy

Cartoons by Martin Angel

British Library Cataloguing-in-Publication Data
A catalogue record for this book is available from the British Library

ISBN 1-90393-844-9

Printed in Singapore